Compact Guide to
Ontario
BIRDS

Contributors:
Andy Bezener, Gregory Kennedy,
Krista Kagume & Carmen Adams

Lone Pine Publishing

© 2005 by Lone Pine Publishing
First printed in 2005   10 9 8 7 6 5
Printed in China

The Publisher: Lone Pine Publishing
10145 – 81 Avenue
Edmonton, AB   T6E 1W9

Website: www.lonepinepublishing.com

Library and Archives Canada Cataloguing in Publication

Compact guide to Ontario birds / Andy Bezener ... [et al.].

Includes bibliographical references and index.
ISBN-13: 978-1-55105-467-4
ISBN-10: 1-55105-467-1

1. Birds--Ontario--Identification. 2. Bird watching--Ontario.
I. Bezener, Andy, 1971-

QL685.5.O5C64 2005   598'.09713   ·   C2004-907161-0

Editorial Director: Nancy Foulds
Project Editor: Carmen Adams
Production Manager: Gene Longson
Book Design: Curt Pillipow
Cover Design: Gerry Dotto
Cover Illustration: Gary Ross
Illustrations: Gary Ross, Ted Nordhagen, Ewa Pluciennik
Egg Photography: Alan Bibby
Layout & Production: Curt Pillipow
Scanning & Digital Film: Elite Lithographers Co.

We acknowledge the financial support of the Government of Canada through the Book Publishing Industry Development Program (BPIDP) for our publishing activities.

PC: 13

Contents

WATERFOWL

Canada Goose
size 107 cm • p. 18

Tundra Swan
size 135 cm • p. 20

Mallard
size 61 cm • p. 22

Blue-winged Teal
size 39 cm • p. 24

Bufflehead
size 36 cm • p. 26

Common Merganser
size 63 cm • p. 28

GROUSE

Ruffed Grouse
size 43 cm • p. 30

Common Loon
size 80 cm • p. 32

Red-necked Grebe
size 50 cm • p. 34

DIVING BIRDS

American White Pelican
size 160 cm • p. 36

Double-crested Cormorant
size 74 cm • p. 38

American Bittern
size 64 cm • p. 40

BITTERNS, HERONS & VULTURES

Great Blue Heron
size 135 cm • p. 42

Turkey Vulture
size 72 cm • p. 44

Osprey
size 60 cm • p. 46

BIRDS OF PREY

Bald Eagle
size 93 cm • p. 48

Northern Harrier
size 51 cm • p. 50

Sharp-shinned Hawk
size 33 cm • p. 52

RAILS & CRANES

Red-tailed Hawk
size 57 cm • p. 54

Peregrine Falcon
size 43 cm • p. 56

Sora
size 23 cm • p. 58

SHOREBIRDS

Sandhill Crane
size 115 cm • p. 60

Killdeer
size 26 cm • p. 62

Lesser Yellowlegs
size 27 cm • p. 64

Spotted Sandpiper
size 19 cm • p. 66

Wilson's Snipe
size 28 cm • p. 68

Wilson's Phalarope
size 23 cm • p. 70

GULLS & TERNS

Bonaparte's Gull
size 33 cm • p. 72

Ring-billed Gull
size 49 cm • p. 74

Herring Gull
size 62 cm • p. 76

PIGEONS & DOVES

Common Tern
size 37 cm • p. 78

Black Tern
size 24 cm • p. 80

Rock Pigeon
size 32 cm • p. 82

OWLS

Mourning Dove
size 31 cm • p. 84

Great Horned Owl
size 55 cm • p. 86

Snowy Owl
size 60 cm • p. 88

OWLS

Northern Saw-whet Owl
size 21 cm • p. 90

Common Nighthawk
size 24 cm • p. 92

Chimney Swift
size 13 cm • p. 94

NIGHTHAWKS, SWIFTS & HUMMINGBIRDS

Ruby-throated Hummingbird
size 9 cm • p. 96

Belted Kingfisher
size 32 cm • p. 98

Yellow-bellied Sapsucker
size 19 cm • p. 100

WOODPECKERS & FLICKERS

Downy Woodpecker
size 17 cm • p. 102

Northern Flicker
size 33 cm • p. 104

Pileated Woodpecker
size 45 cm • p. 106

FLYCATCHERS & KINGBIRDS

Olive-sided Flycatcher
size 19 cm • p. 108

Eastern Kingbird
size 22 cm • p. 110

Northern Shrike
size 25 cm • p. 112

SHRIKES & VIREOS

Red-eyed Vireo
size 15 cm • p. 114

Gray Jay
size 31 cm • p. 116

Blue Jay
size 30 cm • p. 118

JAYS, CROWS & RAVENS

American Crow
size 48 cm • p. 120

Common Raven
size 61 cm • p. 122

Horned Lark
size 18 cm • p. 124

SWALLOWS & LARKS

Purple Martin
size 19 cm • p. 126

Barn Swallow
size 18 cm • p. 128

Black-capped Chickadee
size 14 cm • p. 130

CHICKADEES, NUTHATCHES CREEPERS & WRENS

Red-breasted Nuthatch
size 11 cm • p. 132

Brown Creeper
size 13 cm • p. 134

House Wren
size 12 cm • p. 136

KINGLETS, BLUEBIRDS & ROBINS

Ruby-crowned Kinglet
size 10 cm • p. 138

Eastern Bluebird
size 18 cm • p. 140

American Robin
size 25 cm • p. 142

MIMICS, STARLINGS & WAXWINGS

Gray Catbird
size 23 cm • p. 144

European Starling
size 22 cm • p. 146

Cedar Waxwing
size 18 cm • p. 148

WOOD-WARBLERS & TANAGERS

Yellow Warbler
size 13 cm • p. 150

American Redstart
size 13 cm • p. 152

Common Yellowthroat
size 13 cm • p. 154

SPARROWS

Scarlet Tanager
size 18 cm • p. 156

Chipping Sparrow
size 14 cm • p. 158

Song Sparrow
size 16 cm • p. 160

JUNCOS, CARDINALS & BUNTINGS

Dark-eyed Junco
size 16 cm • p. 162

Northern Cardinal
size 21 cm • p. 164

Indigo Bunting
size 14 cm • p. 166

BLACKBIRDS & ALLIES

Bobolink
size 17 cm • p. 168

Red-winged Blackbird
size 21 cm • p. 170

Eastern Meadowlark
size 24 cm • p. 172

Brown-headed Cowbird
size 18 cm • p. 174

Baltimore Oriole
size 19 cm • p. 176

Purple Finch
size 14 cm • p. 178

FINCHLIKE BIRDS

Common Redpoll
size 13 cm • p. 180

House Sparrow
size 16 cm • p. 182

Introduction

If you have ever admired a songbird's pleasant notes, been fascinated by a soaring hawk or wondered how woodpeckers keep sawdust out of their nostrils, this book is for you. There is so much to discover about birds and their surroundings that birding is becoming one of the fastest growing hobbies on the planet. Many people find it relaxing, while others enjoy its outdoor appeal. Some people see it as a way to reconnect with nature, an opportunity to socialize with like-minded people or a way to monitor the environment.

Whether you are just beginning to take an interest in birds or can already identify many species, there is always more to learn. We've highlighted both the remarkable traits and the more typical behaviours displayed by some of Ontario's most abundant or noteworthy birds. A few live in specialized habitats, but most are common species that you have a good chance of encountering on most outings or in your backyard.

BIRDING IN ONTARIO

More than 400 bird species are found in Ontario, largely because of the geographical and biological diversity of the province. Many birds remain in Ontario during winter because of the moderate climate surrounding the Great Lakes and the warmer southern extreme of the province. (Extreme southwestern Ontario and Northern California share the same latitude.) In addition to the year-round residents, many birds visit our province to breed or just pass through during annual migrations between arctic nesting grounds and southern wintering areas.

Identifying birds in action involves skill, timing and luck. The more you know about a bird—its range, preferred habitat, food preferences and hours and seasons of

Lesser Yellowlegs

activity—the better your chances will be of seeing it. Generally, spring and fall are the busiest birding times. Temperatures are moderate, birds are on the move, tending to nests or migrating, and courtship tunes can be heard. Birds are usually most active in the early morning hours, except in winter when milder temperatures prevail during the day.

Another useful clue for correctly recognizing birds is knowledge of their habitat. Simply put, a bird's habitat is the place where it normally lives. Some birds prefer open water, some birds are found in cattail marshes, others like mature coniferous forest, and still others prefer abandoned agricultural fields overgrown with tall grass and shrubs. Habitats are just like neighbourhoods: if you associate friends with the suburb in which they live, you can easily learn to associate specific birds with their preferred habitats. Only in migration, especially during inclement weather, do some birds leave their usual habitat.

Recognizing birds by their songs and calls can also greatly enhance your birding experience. When experienced birders conduct breeding bird surveys each June, they rely more on their ears than their eyes. There are numerous tapes and CDs that can help you to learn bird songs, and a portable player with headphones can let you quickly compare a live bird with a recording. One way to remember bird songs is to make up words for them. We have given you some of the classic renderings in the accounts that follow, such as *cheerily cheer-up cheerio* for the American Robin. Some of these approximations work better than others; birds often add or delete

American Robin

syllables to their songs and calls. Be aware, also, that songs usually vary from place to place.

Ontario has a long tradition of friendly, recreational birding. Christmas bird counts, breeding bird surveys, nest box programs, migration monitoring and birding lectures and workshops provide a chance for birdwatchers of all levels to interact and share the splendour of birds. Bird hotlines in Ontario provide up-to-date information on the sightings of rarities, which are often easier to relocate than you might think. The following is a brief list of contacts that will help you to get involved:

Federation of Ontario Naturalists (FON)
355 Lesmill Rd.
Don Mills, ON M3B 2W8
Tel: (416) 444-8419
Fax: (416) 444-9866
E-mail: fon@web.net
Web: http://www.ontarionature.org

Ontario Field Ornithologists (OFO)
Box 455, Station R,
Toronto, ON M4G 4E1
E-mail: ofo@interlog.com
Web: http://www.ofo.ca

BIRD HOTLINES
Durham County (Oshawa) (905) 576-2738
Essex County (Windsor) (519) 252-2473
Hamilton (905) 648-9537
Kingston (613) 549-8023
London (519) 457-4593
Ottawa (613) 860-9000
Point Pelee National Park (519) 322-2371
Sault Ste. Marie (705) 256-2790
Simcoe County (Barrie) (705) 739-8585
Toronto & Area (416) 350-3000 (enter 2293)

BIRD LISTING

Many birders list the species they have seen during excursions or at home. It is up to you to decide what kind of list— systematic or casual— you might want to keep. Lists may prove rewarding in unexpected ways, and after you visit a new area, your list becomes a souvenir of your experiences there. Keeping regular, accurate lists of birds in your neighborhood can also be useful for researchers. It is interesting to compare the arrival dates and last sightings of seasonal visitors or to note the first sighting of a new visitor.

BIRD FEEDING

Many people set up bird feeders in their backyard, especially in winter. It is possible to attract specific birds by choosing the right kind of food and style of feeder. Keep your feeder stocked through late spring, because birds have a hard time finding food before the flowers bloom, seeds develop and insects hatch. Contrary to popular opinion, birds do not become dependent on feeders, nor do they subsequently forget to forage naturally. Be sure to clean your feeder and the surrounding area regularly to prevent the spread of disease.

Landscaping your property with native plants is another way of providing natural foods for birds. Flocks of waxwings have a keen eye for red mountain ash berries and hummingbirds enjoy columbine flowers. The cumulative effects of "nature-scaping" urban yards can be a significant step toward habitat conservation. Many good books and web sites about attracting wildlife to your backyard are available.

Red-breasted Nuthatch

NEST BOXES

Another popular way to attract birds is to set out nest boxes, especially for wrens, bluebirds and swallows. Not all birds will use nest boxes: only species that normally use cavities in trees are comfortable in such confined spaces. Larger nest boxes can attract kestrels, owls and cavity-nesting ducks.

ABOUT THE SPECIES ACCOUNTS

This book gives detailed accounts of 83 species of birds that can be expected in Ontario on an annual basis. The order of the birds and their common and scientific names follow the American Ornithologists' Union's *Check-list of North American Birds* (7th ed.) and its supplements.

As well as showing the identifying features of the bird, each species account also attempts to bring the bird to life by describing its various character traits. One of the challenges of birding is that many species look different in spring and

Eastern Bluebird

summer than they do in fall and winter. Many birds have breeding and nonbreeding plumages, and immature birds often look different from their parents. This book does not try to describe or illustrate all the different plumages of a species; instead, it tries to focus on the forms that are most likely to be seen in our area.

ID and **Other ID:** Large illustrations point out prominent field marks that will help you tell each bird apart. The descriptions favour easily understood language instead of technical terms. Some of the most common anatomical features of birds are pointed out in the Glossary illustration (p. 185).

Size: The average length of the bird's body from bill to tail, as well as wingspan, are given and are approximate measurements of the bird as it is seen in nature. The size is sometimes given as a range, because there is variation between individuals, or between males and females.

Voice: You will hear many birds, particularly songbirds, which may remain hidden from view. Memorable paraphrases of distinctive sounds will aid you in identifying a species by ear.

Status: A general comment, such as "common," "uncommon" or "rare," is usually sufficient to describe the relative abundance of a species. Situations are bound to vary somewhat since migratory pulses, seasonal changes and centers of activity tend to concentrate or disperse birds.

Habitat: The habitats listed describe where each species is most commonly found. Because of the freedom flight gives them, birds can turn up in almost any type of habitat. However, they will usually be found in environments that provide the specific food, water, cover and, in some cases, nesting habitat that they need to survive.

Barn Swallow

Similar Birds: Easily confused species are illustrated for each account. If you concentrate on the most relevant field marks, the subtle differences between species can be reduced to easily identifiable traits. Even experienced birders can mistake one species for another.

Nesting: In each species account, a photo of the bird's egg is provided and nest location and structure, clutch size, incubation period and parental duties are discussed. Remember that birding ethics discourage the disturbance of active bird nests. If you disturb a nest, you may drive off the parents during a critical period or expose defenseless young to predators. Because bird egg colours vary, the egg colour description may not always match the photo.

Range Maps: The range map for each species shows the overall range of the species in an average year. Most birds will confine their annual movements to this range, although each year some birds wander beyond their traditional boundaries. The maps show breeding, summer and winter ranges, as well as migratory pathways—areas of the region where birds may appear while en route to nesting or winter habitat. The representations of the pathways do not distinguish high-use migration corridors from areas that are seldom used.

Range Map Symbols

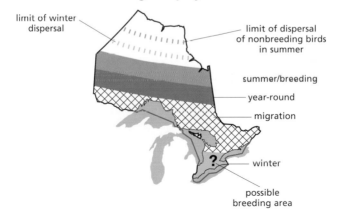

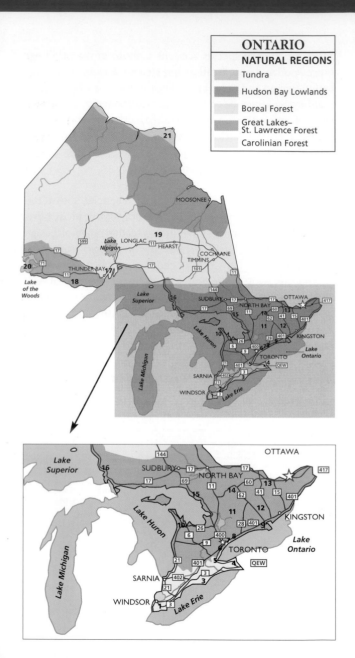

ONTARIO'S TOP BIRDING SITES

Ontario is as diverse as it is large, from the relatively untouched, subarctic forests to the densely populated southern tip. Our province can be separated into five biophysical regions or "bioregions": Carolinian Forest (deciduous forest), Great Lakes–St. Lawrence Forest (mixed forest), Boreal Forest, Hudson Bay Lowland Forest (boreal barrens) and Tundra. The large surface area of the Great Lakes is sometimes considered a sixth bioregion. Each bioregion is composed of a number of different habitats.

There are hundreds, if not thousands, of good birding areas throughout the province. The following areas have been selected to represent a broad range of bird communities and habitats, with an emphasis on accessibility.

1. Point Pelee NP
2. Rondeau PP
3. Long Point PP & Turkey Point PP
4. Niagara River
5. Dundas Marsh
6. Tommy Thompson Park & Toronto Islands
7. Rouge River PP
8. Lynde Shores Conservation Area & Cranberry Marsh
9. Presqu'ile PP
10. The Bruce Peninsula
11. Carden Plain
12. Bon Echo PP
13. Ottawa River PP
14. Algonquin PP
15. Grundy Lake PP & Killarney PP
16. Lake Superior PP
17. Sleeping Giant PP
18. Quetico PP
19. Trans-Canada North (Highway 11)
20. Rainy River & Lake of the Woods
21. Polar Bear PP

PP - Provincial Park
NP - National Park

Canada Goose

Branta canadensis

Canada Geese mate for life and are devoted parents. Unlike most birds, the family stays together for nearly a year, which increases the survival rate of the young. Rescuers who care for injured geese report that these birds readily adopt their human care-givers. However, wild geese can be aggressive, especially when defending young or competing for food. Hissing sounds and low, outstretched necks are signs that you should give these birds some space. • Geese graze on aquatic grasses and sprouts and you can spot them tipping up to grab for aquatic roots and tubers.

Other ID: dark brown upperparts; light brown underparts. *In flight:* flocks fly in V-formation.
Size: L 92–122 cm; W up to 1.8 m.
Voice: loud, familiar *ah-honk*.
Status: common migrant in spring and fall; locally common breeder; occasionally overwinters.
Habitat: lakeshores, riverbanks, ponds, farmlands and city parks.

Similar Birds

Brant

Greater White-fronted Goose

Snow Goose

long, black neck

white "chin strap"

short, black tail

Nesting: usually on the ground; female builds a nest of grasses and mud, lined with down; white eggs are 87 x 58 mm; female incubates 3–8 eggs for 25–28 days; goslings are born in May.

Did You Know?

A migrating Canada Goose will occasionally allow a smaller bird to hitch a ride on its back!

Look For

Several subspecies, each with unique features and varying size, can be found across Ontario.

Tundra Swan
Cygnus columbianus

A wave of Tundra Swans flying overhead is a sight you will never forget. As waters begin to thaw in early March, these noisy swans migrate through our province. They gather at staging areas, where they rest and refuel on waste grain and aquatic vegetation. A good time to visit a staging site is in the evening, when hundreds of swans take flight to feed in nearby fields. Tens of thousands of Tundra Swans migrate over Ontario, but only a handful of pairs actually nest here.

Other ID: slightly concave bill; black feet.
Size: *L* 1.2–1.5 m; *W* 2 m.
Voice: high-pitched, quivering *oo-oo-whoo* repeated in flight.
Status: locally uncommon to abundant migrant; rare summer breeder; rare winter resident.
Habitat: shallow areas of lakes and wetlands, agricultural fields and flooded pastures.

Similar Birds

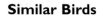

Trumpeter Swan   Mute Swan   Snow Goose

yellow lores

neck is held
straight up

large, black bill

Nesting: on an island or shoreline; nest is a
large mound of vegetation; creamy white eggs
are 107 x 68 mm; female usually incubates 4–5
eggs for 31–32 days.

Did You Know?

Tundra Swans travel over
three months from the
Atlantic Coast to the
Arctic in spring, but spend
only about 114 hours in
the air.

Look For

Huge flocks of Tundra Swans
gather at Long Point, Aylmer
Wildlife Management Area
and Lake St. Clair in the
spring.

Mallard
Anas platyrhynchos

The male Mallard, with his shiny green head and chestnut brown breast, is the classic wild duck. Mallards can be seen year-round, often in flocks and always near open water. These confident ducks have even been spotted dabbling in outdoor swimming pools. • Most people think of the Mallard's quack as the typical duck call, but the Mallard is one of the only ducks that really "quacks." The croak of a male wood frog sounds suspiciously similar to a Mallard's call, so don't be fooled in early spring.

Other ID: orange feet. *Male:* white necklace; black tail feathers curl upward. *Female:* mottled brown overall. *In flight:* dark blue speculum bordered by white.
Size: L 51–71 cm; W 89 cm.
Voice: quacks; female is louder than male.
Status: rare to locally abundant migrant.
Habitat: lakes, wetlands, rivers, city parks, agricultural areas and sewage lagoons.

Similar Birds

Northern Shoveler

American Black Duck

Common Merganser (p. 28)

glossy, green head

yellow bill on male

♂

♀

female's orange
bill is spattered
with black

chestnut brown
breast

Nesting: a grass nest is built on the ground or
under a bush; creamy, grayish or greenish white
eggs are 58 x 41 mm; female incubates 7–10 eggs
for 26–30 days.

Did You Know?

A nesting hen generates
enough body heat to
make the grasses around
her nest grow faster. She
uses them to further con-
ceal her precious nest.

Look For

After breeding, male ducks
experience a short flightless
period, in which they lose
their elaborate plumage and
resemble the females.

Blue-winged Teal
Anas discors

Small, speedy Blue-winged Teals are renowned for their aviation skills. They can be identified by their small size and by the sharp twists and turns they execute in flight. • Blue-winged Teals and other dabbling ducks feed by tipping up their tails and dunking their heads underwater. "Dabblers" have small feet situated near the centre of their bodies. Other ducks, such as scaups, scoters and Buffleheads, dive underwater to feed, propelled by large feet set farther back on their bodies.

Other ID: broad, flat bill. *Male:* white undertail coverts. *Female:* mottled brown overall. *In flight:* blue forewing patch; green speculum.
Size: L 36–41 cm; W 58 cm.
Voice: *Male:* soft *keck-keck-keck*. *Female:* soft quacks.
Status: fairly common to common migrant and breeder; a few may overwinter.
Habitat: shallow lake edges and wetlands; prefers areas with short but dense emergent vegetation.

Similar Birds

Cinnamon Teal   Green-winged Teal   Northern Shoveler

white throat

blue grey head

black-spotted
breast and side

♂

♀

white crescent
on face

Nesting: along a grassy shoreline or in a meadow;
nest is built with grass and considerable amounts
of down; cream-coloured eggs are 46 x 32 mm;
female incubates 8–13 eggs for 23–27 days.

Did You Know?

Blue-winged Teals migrate
farther than most ducks.
They summer as far north
as the Canadian tundra and
winter mainly in Central
and South America.

Look For

The Blue-winged Teal, the
Northern Shoveler and the
Cinnamon Teal are closely
related. They all have broad,
flat bills, pale blue forewings
and green speculums.

Bufflehead
Bucephala albeola

The tiny Bufflehead might be the first diving duck you learn to identify. With its simple, bold plumage, this abundant duck resembles few other species. The striking white patch on the rear of the male's head stands out, even at a distance. • Buffleheads often nest in tree cavities, using abandoned woodpecker nests or natural holes. After hatching, the ducklings remain in the nest chamber for up to three days before jumping out and tumbling to the ground.

Other ID: short, grey bill; short neck. *Male:* dark back; white neck and underparts. *Female:* dark brown head and upperparts; light brown sides. *In flight:* white speculum.
Size: L 33–38 cm; W 53 cm.
Voice: *Male:* growling call. *Female:* harsh quack.
Status: common to locally abundant migrant and winter visitor on the Great Lakes; rare to uncommon breeder.
Habitat: open water on lakes, large ponds and rivers.

Similar Birds

Hooded Merganser

Barrow's Goldeneye

Common Goldeneye

white, oval
ear patch

♀

iridescent dark green
or purple head usually
appears black

white wedge
on back
of head

♂

Nesting: in a tree cavity; often near water;
pale buff to cream eggs are 51 x 37 mm;
female incubates 6–12 eggs for 28–33 days.

Did You Know?

Diving ducks have smaller
wings than dabbling ducks,
so they require a longer
stretch of water for
takeoff.

Look For

In winter, look for
Buffleheads on the Great
Lakes, diving for molluscs
such as snails. With luck, you
might even see a whole flock
dive at once.

Common Merganser
Mergus merganser

The ponderous Common Merganser must run along the surface of the water, beating its heavy wings to gain sufficient lift to take flight. Once up and away, this large duck flies arrow-straight and low over the water, making broad, sweeping turns to follow meandering rivers and lake shorelines.
• Common Mergansers are highly social and often gather in large groups during migration. In winter, any source of open water with a fish-filled shoal will support good numbers of these skilled divers.

Other ID: large, elongated body; serrated bill. *Male:* white body plumage; black stripe on back; dark eyes. *Female:* grey body; orangy eyes.
Size: *L* 56–69 cm; *W* 86 cm.
Voice: *Male:* harsh *uig-a*, like a guitar twang. *Female:* harsh *karr karr*.
Status: rare to common breeder; uncommon to common in winter.
Habitat: large rivers and deep lakes.

Similar Birds

Red-breasted Merganser

Common Goldeneye

Common Loon (p.32)

glossy, green head without crest

blood red bill and feet

rusty neck and crested head

orange bill

clean white "chin" and breast

Nesting: in a tree cavity 15–20 ft above the ground; occasionally on the ground, on a cliff ledge or in a large nest box; usually close to water; pale buff eggs are 66 x 46 mm; female incubates 8–11 eggs for 30–35 days.

Did You Know?

The Common Merganser is the most widespread and abundant merganser in North America. It also occurs in Europe and Asia.

Look For

In flight, the Common Merganser has shallow wing beats and an arrowlike, compressed body.

Ruffed Grouse
Bonasa umbellus

If you hear a loud "boom" echoing through the forest, you are likely listening to a Ruffed Grouse "drumming" to announce his territory. Every spring, and occasionally in fall, the male grouse struts along a fallen log with his tail fanned and his neck feathers ruffed, beating the air periodically with accelerating wingstrokes. • In winter, scales grow out along the sides of the Ruffed Grouse's feet, creating temporary "snow-shoes." Though many birds can walk on snow, only grouse and ptarmigan have this specialized feature.

Other ID: mottled, grey brown overall; grey or reddish-barred tail. *Female:* incomplete subterminal tail band.
Size: L 38–48 cm; W 56 cm.
Voice: courting male drums to produce deep, accelerating booms.
Status: common year-round resident.
Habitat: deciduous and mixed forests and riparian woodlands; favours young, second-growth stands with birch and poplar.

Similar Birds

Spruce Grouse

Sharp-tailed Grouse

small, pointed head crest

black feathers on sides
of lower neck

tail has broad, dark, subterminal
band and white tip

♂ *grey morph*

Nesting: in a shallow depression, often beside
boulders or under a log; buff-coloured eggs are
40 x 30 mm; female incubates 9–12 eggs for
23–25 days.

Did You Know?

During winter, Ruffed
Grouse bury themselves
in snowbanks to keep
warm.

Look For

As a potential threat
approaches, Ruffed Grouse
stand still to camouflage
themselves against the forest
floor. For every grouse seen,
many more go unnoticed.

Common Loon
Gavia immer

When the haunting call of the Common Loon pierces a still evening, cottagers know that summer has begun. Loons actually have several different calls. Frightened loons give a laughing distress call; separated pairs seem to wail *where aaare you?* and groups give soft, cohesive hoots as they fly.
• Common Loons are well suited to their aquatic lifestyle. Most birds have hollow bones, but loons have solid bones that reduce their buoyancy and make it easier for them to dive.

Other ID: *Breeding:* stout, thick, black bill; white breast and underparts. *Nonbreeding:* much duller plumage; sandy brown back; light underparts. *In flight:* long wings beat constantly; hunch-backed appearance; legs trail behind tail.
Size: L 71–89 cm; W 1.2–1.5 m.
Voice: alarm call is a quavering tremolo; also wails, hoots and yodels.
Status: common migrant; fairly common breeder; rare winter resident.
Habitat: large lakes, often with islands that provide undisturbed shorelines for nesting.

Similar Birds

Red-throated Loon

Pacific Loon

nonbreeding

green black head

red eyes

black-and-white
"checkerboard"
upperparts

white "necklace"

breeding

Nesting: on a muskrat lodge, small island or
shoreline; nest is a mound of aquatic vegetation;
darkly spotted, olive brown eggs are 90 x 57 mm;
both parents incubate 1–3 eggs for 24–31 days
and raise young.

Did You Know?

Hungry loons will chase
fish to depths of 55
metres—as deep as an
Olympic-sized swimming
pool is long.

Look For

Rear-placed legs make walk-
ing on land awkward for
these birds. The word "loon"
is probably derived from the
Scandinavian word *lom,* which
means "clumsy person."

Red-necked Grebe
Podiceps grisegena

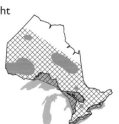

As evening settles over a wetland, the laughing calls of courting Red-necked Grebes signal the beginning of a new spring breeding season.

nonbreeding

Although Red-necked Grebes are not as vocally refined as loons, few loons can match the energy of a pair of grebes. In late May, their wild laughter often lasts through the night.
• Grebes have individually webbed, or "lobed," feet. The three forward-facing toes have special flanges that are not connected to the other toes. • These birds feed, sleep and court on water.

Other ID: *Breeding:* black upperparts; light underparts; dark eyes. *Nonbreeding:* greyish white foreneck, "chin" and "cheek."
Size: *L* 43–56 cm; *W* 61 cm.
Voice: often-repeated, laughlike, excited *ah-ooo ah-ooo ah-ooo ah-ah-ah-ah-ah.*
Status: fairly common migrant; rare breeder; a few may overwinter.
Habitat: open, deep lakes.

Similar Birds

Horned Grebe

Pied-billed Grebe

Eared Grebe

black crown

whitish "cheek"

rusty neck

straight, heavy bill
is dark above and
yellow underneath

breeding

Nesting: usually singly or in loose colonies; floating
platform nest is anchored to pondweeds; white
eggs, often stained by vegetation, are 56 x 36 mm;
both parents incubate 4–5 eggs for 20–23 days.

Did You Know?

It is thought that grebes
eat feathers to line their
digestive tracts, protect-
ing their organs from
sharp fish bones or
parasites.

Look For

Grebes carry their newly
hatched, striped young on
their backs. The young are
able to stay aboard even
when the parents dive
underwater.

American White Pelican
Pelecanus erythrorhynchos

This majestic wetland bird is one of only a few bird species that feeds cooperatively. A group of pelicans will herd fish into a school, then dip their bucketlike bills into the water to capture their prey. In a single scoop, a pelican can trap over 12 litres of water and fish in its bill, which is about two to three times as much as its stomach can hold. This impressive feat inspired Dixon Lanier Merritt to write: "A wonderful bird is a pelican. His bill will hold more than his belican!"

Other ID: *Breeding:* small, keeled plate develops on upper mandible; pale yellow crest on back of head.
Size: *L* 1.4–1.8 m; *W* 2.8 m.
Voice: generally quiet; rarely issues piglike grunts.
Status: locally abundant breeder; rare post-breeding wanderer from June to December.
Habitat: large lakes or rivers.

Similar Birds

Tundra Swan (p. 20)　　　Trumpeter Swan　　　Mute Swan

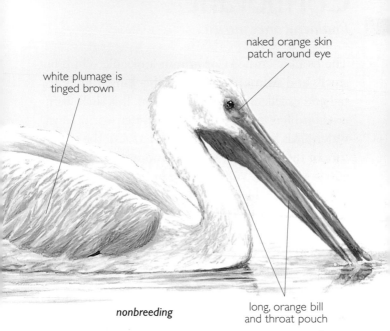

naked orange skin
patch around eye

white plumage is
tinged brown

nonbreeding

long, orange bill
and throat pouch

Nesting: colonial; on a bare, low-lying island; scrape nest is unlined or lined with debris; dull white eggs, often with some streaking or discolouration are 87 x 56 mm; pair incubates 2 eggs for 29–36 days.

Did You Know?

The feathers on a pelican's wing tips are black and have a pigment called melanin that doesn't wear in the wind.

Look For

When pelicans fly into the wind, they often stay close to the surface of the water. When the wind is at their backs, they will fly much higher.

Double-crested Cormorant

Phalacrocorax auritus

The Double-crested Cormorant looks like a bird but smells and swims like a fish. With a long, rudderlike tail and excellent underwater vision, this slick-feathered bird has mastered the underwater world. Most water birds have waterproof feathers, but the structure of the Double-crested Cormorant's feathers allows water in. "Wettable" feathers make this bird less buoyant, which in turn makes it a better diver. The Double-crested Cormorant also has sealed nostrils for diving, and therefore must fly with its bill open.

Other ID: all-black body; blue eyes. *Immature:* brown upperparts; buff throat and breast; yellowish throat patch. *In flight:* rapid wingbeats; kinked neck.
Size: L 66–81 cm; W 1.3 m.
Voice: generally quiet; may issue piglike grunts or croaks, especially near nest colonies.
Status: uncommon to locally common in summer; a few may overwinter.
Habitat: large lakes and large, meandering rivers; Great Lakes.

Similar Birds

Canada Goose (p. 18)

Common Loon (p. 32)

fine, black plumes trail from "eyebrows"

thin bill, hooked at tip

orange yellow throat pouch

juvenile

long, crooked neck

breeding

Nesting: colonial; on an island or high in a tree; platform nest is made of sticks and guano; bluish white eggs are 51 x 38 mm; both sexes incubate 2–7 eggs for 25–30 days.

Did You Know?

Japanese fishermen sometimes use cormorants on leashes to catch fish. This traditional method of fishing is called *Ukai*.

Look For

Double-crested Cormorants often perch on trees or piers with their wings partially spread. Lacking oil glands, they use the wind to dry their feathers.

American Bittern
Botaurus lentiginosus

The American Bittern's deep, pumping call is as common in a spring marsh as the sound of croaking of frogs, but this well-camouflaged bird remains well hidden. When an intruder approaches, the bittern freezes with its bill pointed skyward—its vertically streaked, brown plumage blends perfectly with the surrounding marsh. In most cases, intruders simply pass by without ever noticing the bird. An American Bittern will adopt this reedlike position even in an open field, apparently unaware that a lack of cover betrays its presence!

Other ID: brown upperparts; rich buff flanks and sides; white underparts; yellow legs and feet; black outer wings; short tail.
Size: *L* 59–69 cm; *W* 1.1 m.
Voice: deep, slow, resonant, repetitive *pomp-er-lunk* or *onk-a-BLONK;* most often heard in the evening or at night.
Status: rare to fairly common migrant and breeder; a few may overwinter.
Habitat: productive wetlands and lake edges with tall, dense sedges, bulrushes or cattails.

Similar Birds

Least Bittern

Look For

Late mornings and early afternoons are the best times to spot this secretive bird. It sways its head, mimicing surrounding vegetation, while hunting.

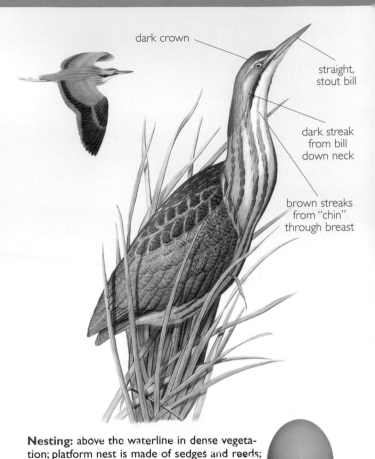

dark crown

straight, stout bill

dark streak from bill down neck

brown streaks from "chin" through breast

Nesting: above the waterline in dense vegetation; platform nest is made of sedges and reeds; separate paths often lead to nest; pale olive or buff eggs are 49 x 37 mm; female incubates 3–5 eggs for 24–28 days.

Did You Know?

American Bittern populations across much of North America are declining. The decrease in numbers is attributed to habitat loss, chemical contamination of wetlands and human disturbance.

Great Blue Heron
Ardea herodias

The long-legged Great Blue Heron has a stealthy, often motionless hunting strategy. It waits for a fish or frog to approach, spears the prey with its bill, then flips its catch into the air and swallows it whole. Herons usually hunt near water, but they also stalk fields and meadows in search of rodents.
• Great Blue Herons settle in communal treetop nests called rookeries. Nesting herons are sensitive to human disturbance, so observe this bird's behaviour from a distance.

Other ID: blue grey overall; long, dark legs. *Breeding:* richer colours; plumes streak from crown and throat. *In flight:* black upperwing tips; neck folds back over shoulders; legs trail behind body; slow, steady wingbeats.
Size: L 1.3–1.4 m; W 1.8 m.
Voice: quiet away from the nest; occasional harsh *frahnk frahnk frahnk* during takeoff.
Status: fairly common migrant and breeder; a few may overwinter.
Habitat: forages along edges of rivers, lakes, marshes, fields and wet meadows.

Similar Birds

Little Blue Heron

Black-crowned
Night-Heron

Great Egret

black plumes above eye

straight, yellow bill

long, curving neck with black markings on throat

chestnut brown thighs

Nesting: colonial; adds to stick platform nest over years; nest width can reach 1.2 m; pale bluish green eggs are 64 x 45 mm; pair incubates 4–7 eggs for approximately 28 days.

Did You Know?

The Great Blue Heron is the tallest of all herons and egrets in North America.

Look For

In flight, the Great Blue Heron folds its neck back over its shoulders in an S-shape. Similar-looking cranes stretch their necks out when flying.

Turkey Vulture
Cathartes aura

Turkey Vultures are intelligent, playful and social birds. Groups live and sleep together in large trees, or roosts. Some roost sites are over a century old and have been used by the same family of vultures for several generations. • The scientific name *Cathartes aura* means "cleanser" and refers to this bird's affinity for carrion. A vulture's bill and feet are much less powerful than those of eagles, hawks or falcons, which kill live prey. The Turkey Vulture's red, featherless head may appear grotesque, but this adaptation allows the bird to stay relatively clean while feeding on messy carcasses.

Other ID: *Immature:* grey head. *In flight:* head appears small; silver grey flight feathers; wings are held in a shallow "V"; rocks from side-to-side when soaring.
Size: *L* 65–80 cm; *W* 1.7–1.8 m.
Voice: generally silent; occasionally produces a hiss or grunt if threatened.
Status: uncommon to fairly common migrant and breeder; a few may over-winter.
Habitat: usually flies over open country, shorelines or roads; rarely over forests.

Similar Birds

Black Vulture

Golden Eagle

Bald Eagle (p. 48)

bare, red head

pale, hooked bill

Nesting: in a cave, crevice, log or among boulders; no nest material; dull white eggs, irregularly marked with brown or purple, are 71 x 49 mm; pair incubates 2 eggs for up to 41 days.

Did You Know?

A threatened Turkey Vulture will either play dead or throw up. The vomit's odour repulses attackers, much like the odour of a skunk's spray.

Look For

No other bird uses updrafts and thermals in flight as well as the Turkey Vulture. Pilots have reported seeing vultures soaring at 6000 m.

Osprey

Pandion haliaetus

The large and powerful Osprey is almost always found near water. While hunting for fish, this bird hovers in the air before hurling itself in a dramatic headfirst dive. An instant before striking the water, it rights itself and thrusts its feet forward to grasp its prey. The Osprey has specialized feet for gripping slippery prey—two toes face forward, two face backward and all are covered with sharp spines. • The Osprey is one of the most widely distributed birds in the world—it is found on every continent except Antarctica.

Other ID: yellow eyes; light crown. *Male:* all-white throat. *Female:* fine, dark "necklace." *In flight:* long wings are held in a shallow "M"; dark "wrist" patches; brown and white tail bands.
Size: L 56–64 cm; W 1.7–1.8 m.
Voice: series of melodious ascending whistles: *chewk-chewk-chewk;* also a familiar *kip-kip-kip.*
Status: uncommon to fairly common migrant and breeder; a few may overwinter.
Habitat: lakes and slow-flowing rivers and streams.

Similar Birds

Bald Eagle (p. 48)

Rough-legged Hawk

dark eye line

long wings
extend past tail

grey bill and feet

♂

Nesting: on a treetop or artificial structure,
usually near water; massive stick nest is reused
annually; yellowish, brown-blotched eggs are
61 x 46 mm; pair incubates 2–4 eggs for 38 days.

Did You Know?

The Osprey's dark eye
line blocks the glare of
the sun on the water,
enabling it to spot fish
near the water's surface.

Look For

Ospreys build bulky nests on
high, artificial structures such
as communication towers
and utility poles, or on buoys
and channel markers over
water.

Bald Eagle
Haliaeetus leucocephalus

Part of the sea eagle group, the majestic Bald Eagle feeds mostly on fish and is often found near water. While soaring hundreds of metres high in the air, an eagle can spot fish swimming under-water and small rodents scurrying through the grass. Eagles also scavenge carrion and steal food from other birds. • Bald Eagles do not mature until their fourth or fifth year—only then will they develop the characteristic white head and tail plumage.

immature

Other ID: *1st-year:* dark overall; dark bill; some white in underwings. *2nd-year:* dark "bib"; white in underwings. *3rd-year:* mostly white plumage; yellow at base of bill; yellow eyes. *4th-year:* light head with dark facial streak; variable pale-and-dark plumage; yellow bill; paler eyes.
Size: L 76–109 cm; W 1.7–2.4 m.
Voice: thin, weak squeal or gull-like cackle: *kleek-kik-kik-kik* or *kah-kah-kah*.
Status: rare to locally uncommon migrant and breeder; rare but regular local winter resident.
Habitat: large lakes and rivers.

Similar Birds

Golden Eagle

Osprey (p. 46)

white head
and tail

yellow bill

yellow feet

adult

Nesting: in a tree; usually, but not always, near water; huge stick nest is often reused for many years; white eggs are 71 x 54 mm; pair incubates 1–3 eggs for 34–36 days.

Did You Know?

Bald Eagles add sticks to their nests to renew pair bonds. Nests can be up to 4.5 m in diameter, the largest of any North American bird.

Look For

In winter, ducks gather on industrial ponds or other ice-free waters, unknowingly providing an easy meal for hungry Bald Eagles.

Northern Harrier
Circus cyaneus

With its prominent white rump and distinctive slightly upturned wings, the Northern Harrier may be the easiest raptor to identify in flight. Unlike other midsized birds, it often flies close to the ground, relying on sudden surprise attacks to capture prey. • The courtship flight of the Northern Harrier is a spectacle worth watching in spring. The male climbs almost vertically in the air, then stalls and plummets in a reckless dive toward the ground. At the last second he saves himself with a hairpin turn that sends him skyward again.

Other ID: *Male:* blue grey to silver grey upperparts; white underparts; indistinct tail bands, except for 1 dark subterminal band. *Female:* dark brown upperparts; streaky brown-and-buff underparts. *In flight:* long wings and tail; black wing tips; white rump.
Size: *L* 41–61 cm; *W* 1.1–1.2 m.
Voice: generally quiet; high-pitched *ke-ke-ke-ke-ke-ke* near the nest or during courtship.
Status: uncommon to common migrant and breeder; rare winter resident.
Habitat: open country, including fields, wet meadows, cattail marshes, bogs and croplands.

Similar Birds

Rough-legged Hawk

Red-tailed Hawk (p. 54)

facial disc

♂

yellow legs

long,
dark-banded tail

♀

Nesting: on the ground; usually in tall vegetation or on a raised mound; shallow depression is lined with grass, sticks and cattails; bluish white eggs are 47 × 36 mm; female incubates 4–6 eggs for 30–32 days.

Did You Know?

Britain's Royal Air Force was so impressed by the Northern Harrier's manoeuvrability that it named the Harrier aircraft after this bird.

Look For

The Northern Harrier's owl-like, parabolic facial disc enhances its hearing, allowing this bird to hunt by sound as well as sight.

Sharp-shinned Hawk

Accipiter striatus

After a successful hunt, the small Sharp-shinned Hawk often perches on a favourite "plucking post" with its meal in its razor-sharp talons. Sharpies are members of the *Accipter* genus, or woodland hawks, and prey almost exclusively on small birds. Their short, rounded wings, long, rudderlike tails and flap-and-glide flight pattern allow them to manoeuvre through the forest at high speed.

• When delivering food to his nestlings, a male Sharp-shinned Hawk takes care not to disturb his mate—she is typically one-third larger than he is and notoriously short-tempered.

Other ID: red eyes; blue grey back and upperwings.
In flight: short, rounded wings; dark barring on flight feathers; flap-and-glide flight pattern.
Size: *Male:* L 25–30 cm; W 51–61 cm.
Female: L 30–36 cm; W 61–71 cm.
Voice: usually silent; intense, repeated
kik-kik-kik-kik during the breeding season.
Status: common migrant; uncommon breeder; rare in winter.
Habitat: dense to semi-open forests and large woodlots; occasionally along rivers and in urban areas; favours bogs and dense, moist, forests for nesting.

Similar Birds

Cooper's Hawk

American Kestrel

Merlin

blue grey crown

red horizontal bars
on underparts

immature

long, heavily barred,
square-tipped tail

Nesting: in a conifer tree; builds a new stick nest or uses an abandoned crow nest; brown-blotched, dull white eggs are 38 x 30 mm; female incubates 4–5 eggs for 34–35 days; male feeds the female during incubation.

Did You Know?

As it ages, the Sharp-shinned Hawk's bright yellow eyes become red. This change may signal full maturity to potential mates.

Look For

During winter, Sharp-shinned Hawks may visit backyard bird feeders to prey on feeding sparrows and finches.

Red-tailed Hawk
Buteo jamaicensis

Take an afternoon drive through the country and look for Red-tailed Hawks soaring above the fields. Red-tails are the most common hawks in Ontario, especially in the southwestern agricultural areas.
• In warm weather, the hawks use thermals and updrafts to soar. These pockets of rising air provide substantial lift, which allows migrating hawks to fly for almost 3 kilometres without flapping their wings once. On cooler days, resident Red-tails perch on exposed tree limbs, fence posts or utility poles to scan for prey.

Other ID: brown eyes. *In flight:* fan-shaped tail; light underwing flight feathers with faint barring; dark leading edge on underside of wing.
Size: *Male:* L 46–58 cm; W 1.2–1.5 m.
Female: L 51–64 cm; W 1.2–1.5 m.
Voice: powerful, descending scream: *keeearrrr.*
Status: common to abundant year-round.
Habitat: open country with some trees; also roadsides, fields or woodlots.

Similar Birds

Rough-legged Hawk

Broad-winged Hawk

Red-shouldered Hawk

Swainson's Hawk

dark upperparts
with some white
highlights

dark brown band of
streaks across belly

red tail

Nesting: in woodlands adjacent to open habitat;
bulky stick nest is enlarged each year; brown-
blotched, whitish eggs are 59 x 47 mm; pair
incubates 2–4 eggs for 28–35 days.

Did You Know?

The Red-tailed Hawk's
piercing call is often
paired with the image of
an eagle in TV commer-
cials and movies.

Look For

Courting pairs will dive at
each other, lock talons and
tumble toward the earth.
They break away at the last
second, just before hitting
the ground.

Peregrine Falcon
Falco peregrinus

Nothing causes more panic in a flock of ducks or shorebirds than a hunting Peregrine Falcon. This powerful raptor matches every twist and turn the flock makes, then dives to strike a lethal blow.

• Peregrine Falcons represent a successful conservation effort. In the 1960s, the pesticide DDT caused peregrines to lay eggs with thin shells that broke easily. Peregrine populations declined dramatically until DDT was banned in North America in 1972. Since then, hundreds of captive-bred peregrines have been successfully reintroduced to the wild.

Other ID: blue grey back; yellow feet and cere. *In flight:* pointed wings; long, narrow, dark-banded tail.
Size: *Male:* L 38–43 cm; W 94–109 cm. *Female:* L 43–48 cm; W 1.1–1.2 m.
Voice: loud, harsh, continuous *cack-cack-cack-cack-cack* near the nest site.
Status: rare to uncommon migrant; very rare breeder.
Habitat: lakeshores, river valleys, river mouths, urban areas and open fields.

Similar Birds

Gyrfalcon

Merlin

dark "helmet"

white to buff
"chin" and throat

prominent, light
underparts with
dark, fine spotting
and flecking

Nesting: usually on a rocky cliff or cutbank; nest site is often reused and littered with prey remains; white eggs with reddish, brownish or purple blotches are 53 x 41 mm; pair incubates 3–5 eggs for 32–34 days.

Did You Know?

The Peregrine Falcon is the world's fastest bird. In a headfirst dive, it can reach speeds of up to 350 km per hour.

Look For

A pair of peregrines will sometimes nest on the ledge of a tall building, right in the middle of an urban area.

Sora
Porzana carolina

Soras have small bodies and large, chickenlike feet. Even without webbed feet, these unique creatures swim quite well over short distances. • Two rising *or-Ah or-Ah* whistles followed by a strange, descending whinny indicate that Soras are nearby. Although the Sora is the most common and widespread rail species in North America, it is seldom seen. This secretive bird prefers to remain hidden in dense marshland, but it will occasionally venture into the shallows to search for aquatic insects and molluscs.

Other ID: *Nonbreeding:* less black on face and throat. *Immature:* no black on face; bill is darker; paler underparts.
Size: *L* 20–25 cm; *W* 35 cm.
Voice: alarm call is a sharp *keek;* courtship song begins *or-Ah or-Ah* followed by a maniacal, descending *weee-weee-weee.*
Status: uncommon to common migrant and breeder; may overwinter.
Habitat: wetlands with abundant emergent cattails, bulrushes, sedges and grasses.

Similar Birds

Virginia Rail

King Rail

Yellow Rail

brown, white-speckled back and upper wings

short, yellow bill

black face, throat and foreneck

grey neck and breast

long, greenish legs

breeding

Nesting: usually over water or in a wet meadow; well-built basket nest is made of grass and aquatic vegetation; darkly speckled, buff or olive buff eggs are 31 x 22 mm; pair incubates 10–12 eggs for 18–20 days.

Did You Know?

Literally as "thin as a rail," the Sora has a very narrow body that allows it to squeeze through thick stands of cattails.

Look For

The Sora has long legs, a stumpy body and almost no neck. It bustles through the shallows, darting in and out of the reeds.

Sandhill Crane
Grus canadensis

The Sandhill Crane's deep, rattling call can be heard long before this bird passes overhead. Its coiled trachea alters the pitch of its voice, making it sound louder and carry farther. • At first glance, large, V-shaped flocks of Sandhill Cranes can look like flocks of Canada Geese, but the cranes often soar and circle in the air, and they do not honk like geese. • Cranes mate for life and reinforce pair bonds each spring with an elaborate courtship dance. The ritual looks much like human dancing, which may seem like a strange comparison until you witness the spectacle firsthand.

Other ID: grey overall; long, straight bill; dark legs; plumage is often stained rusty red from iron oxides in water.
Size: L 1–1.3 m; W 1.8–2.1 m.
Voice: loud, resonant, rattling: *gu-rrroo gu-rrroo gurrroo.*
Status: rare to locally uncommon migrant and breeder; a few may over-winter.
Habitat: open ground, fields, lakeshores, sandy beaches, mudflats, gravel streambeds, wet meadows and grasslands.

Similar Birds

Whooping Crane Great Blue Heron (p. 42)

naked, red crown

white "cheek" and "chin"

long neck

grey overall

Nesting: in the water or along the shoreline; on a large mound of aquatic vegetation; brown-blotched, buff eggs are 94 x 60 mm; pair incubates 2 eggs for 29–32 days; egg hatching is staggered.

Did You Know?

Sandhill Cranes are sensitive nesters, so prefer to raise their young in areas isolated from human disturbance.

Look For

In Ontario, the Sault Ste. Marie area is a good place to spot cranes in the spring. Most Sandhills seen in our province are migrants, and breeding cranes are rare.

Killdeer
Charadrius vociferus

The boisterous Killdeer always attracts attention. It is a gifted actor, well known for its "broken wing" distraction display. When an intruder wanders too close to its nest, it is greeted by an adult, who cries piteously while dragging a wing and stumbling about as if injured. Most predators take the bait and follow, and once the Killdeer has lured the predator far away from its nest, it miraculously recovers from the injury and flies off with a loud call.

Other ID: brown head; white neck band; brown back and upperwings; white underparts; rufous rump. *Immature:* downy; only 1 breast band.
Size: L 23–28 cm; W 61 cm.
Voice: loud and distinctive *kill-dee kill-dee kill-deer;* variations include *deer-deer.*
Status: common to abundant migrant and breeder; a few may overwinter.
Habitat: open ground, fields, lakeshores, sandy beaches, mudflats, gravel streambeds, wet meadows and grasslands.

Similar Birds

Semipalmated Plover

Piping Plover

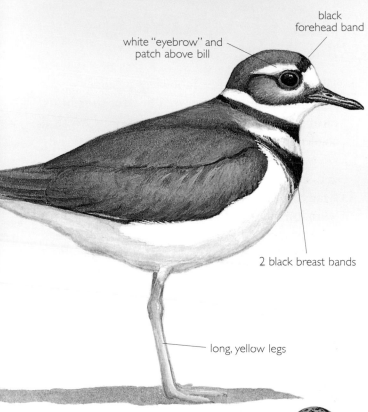

black
forehead band

white "eyebrow" and
patch above bill

2 black breast bands

long, yellow legs

Nesting: on open ground, in a shallow, usually unlined depression; heavily marked, creamy buff eggs are 36 x 27 mm; pair incubates 4 eggs for 24–28 days; may raise 2 broods.

Did You Know?

In spring, you might hear a European Starling imitate the vocal Killdeer's call.

Look For

The Killdeer has adapted well to urbanization, and inhabits golf courses, farms, fields and abandoned industrial areas as often as shorelines.

Lesser Yellowlegs
Tringa flavipes

The "tattle-tale" Lesser Yellowlegs is the self-appointed sentinel in a mixed flock of shorebirds, raising the alarm at the first sign of a threat. • It is challenging to discern Lesser Yellowlegs and Greater Yellowlegs in the field, but with practice, you will notice that the Lesser's bill is finer, straighter and about as long as its head is wide. With long legs and wings, the Lesser appears slimmer and taller than the Greater, and it is more commonly seen in flocks. Finally, the Lesser Yellowlegs emits a pair of peeps, while the Greater Yellowlegs peeps three times.

Other ID: subtle, dark eye line; light lores.
Size: L 25–28 cm; W 61 cm.
Voice: typically a high-pitched pair of *tew* notes; noisiest on breeding grounds.
Status: common to abundant migrant and breeder; rare in winter.
Habitat: *Breeding:* grassy ponds and open forest. *In migration:* shorelines of lakes, rivers, marshes and ponds.

Similar Birds

Willet

Greater Yellowlegs

Solitary Sandpiper

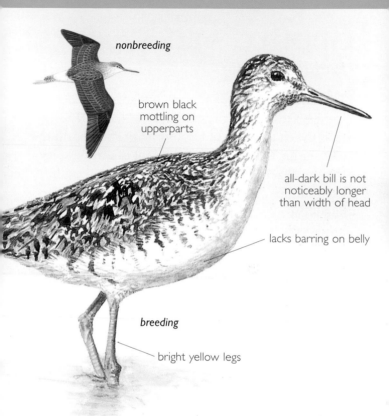

nonbreeding

brown black mottling on upperparts

all-dark bill is not noticeably longer than width of head

lacks barring on belly

breeding

bright yellow legs

Nesting: in open muskeg or a natural forest opening; in a depression on a dry mound lined with leaves and grass; darkly blotched, buff to olive eggs are 42 x 29 mm; pair incubates 4 eggs for 22–23 days.

Did You Know?

Lesser Yellowlegs and Greater Yellowlegs both nest in the muskeg of the Hudson Bay Lowlands, but Lessers tend to nest on higher, drier terrain.

Look For

The Lesser Yellowlegs pays only a brief visit to Ontario in spring, but its fall migration period lasts from mid-July to mid-October.

Spotted Sandpiper
Actitis macularius

The female Spotted Sandpiper, unlike most other female birds, lays her eggs and leaves the male to tend the clutch. Free of responsibility, she flies off to mate again. Only about one percent of birds display this unusual breeding strategy known as polyandry. Each summer, the female can lay up to four clutches and is capable of producing 20 eggs. As the season progresses, however, available males become harder to find. Come August, there may be seven females for every available male.

Other ID: teeters almost continuously. *Nonbreeding* and *immature:* pure white breast, foreneck and throat; brown bill; dull yellow legs. *In flight:* white upperwing stripe.
Size: *L* 18–20 cm; *W* 38 cm.
Voice: sharp, crisp *eat-wheat, eat-wheat, wheat-wheat-wheat-wheat.*
Status: common migrant and breeder.
Habitat: shorelines, gravel beaches, ponds, marshes, alluvial wetlands, rivers, streams, swamps and sewage lagoons; occasionally seen in cultivated fields.

Similar Birds

Solitary Sandpiper

Look For

Spotted Sandpipers bob their tails constantly on shore and fly with rapid, shallow, stiff wingbeats close to the water's surface.

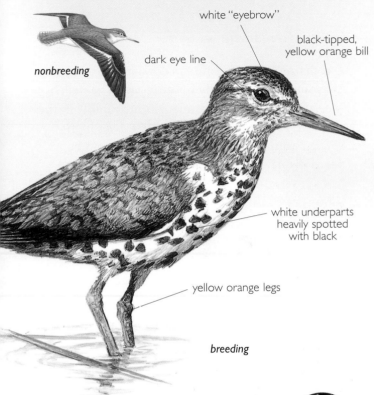

white "eyebrow"

black-tipped,
yellow orange bill

dark eye line

nonbreeding

white underparts
heavily spotted
with black

yellow orange legs

breeding

Nesting: usually near water; sheltered by vegetation, shallow scrape is lined with grass; darkly blotched, creamy buff eggs are 33 x 24 mm; male incubates 4 eggs for 20–24 days and raises the young.

Did You Know?

The Spotted Sandpiper is common and widespread across North and Central America. It isn't particular in its choice of habitat or food. It will live almost anywhere that is close to water, and it eats a wide variety of aquatic and terrestrial invertebrates.

Wilson's Snipe
Gallinago delicata

A courting Wilson's Snipe makes an eerie, winnowing sound, like a rapidly hooting owl. The male's specialized outer tail feathers vibrate rapidly in the air as he performs daring, headfirst dives high above a wetland. During spring, snipes can be heard displaying day and night. • When flushed from cover, these birds perform a series of aerial zigzags to confuse predators. Because of this habit, hunters who were skilled enough to shoot snipes became known as "snipers," a term later adopted by the military.

Other ID: unmarked, white belly; relatively short legs. *In flight:* quick zigzags on takeoff.
Size: L 27–29 cm; W 46 cm.
Voice: in flight, courtship song is an eerie, accelerating *woo-woo-woo-woo-woo-woo;* often sings *wheat wheat wheat* from an elevated perch; alarm call is a nasal *scaip.*
Status: fairly common to common migrant and breeder; a few may overwinter near water.
Habitat: cattail and bulrush marshes, sedge meadows, poorly drained floodplains, bogs and fens; willow and red-osier dogwood tangles.

Similar Birds

Short-billed Dowitcher

Long-billed Dowitcher

American Woodcock

dark eye stripe

heavily striped head, back and neck

long, sturdy, bicoloured bill

dark barring on breast and flanks

Nesting: usually in dry grass; nest is made of grass, moss and leaves; darkly marked, olive buff to brown eggs are 39 x 28 mm; female incubates 4 eggs for 18–20 days.

Did You Know?

Both parents raise the snipe nestlings, often splitting the brood, with each parent caring for half the chicks.

Look For

A snipe often plunges its entire head underwater while probing the shallows for tasty aquatic critters.

Wilson's Phalarope
Phalaropus tricolor

Phalaropes are like wind-up toys: they spin and whirl about in tight circles, stirring up aquatic insects and small crustaceans. Then, with needle-like bills, they pluck their prey from the water as it funnels toward the surface. • While incubating the eggs, the male phalarope sheds the feathers on his belly, and develops a thick skin on his underside. This "brood patch" swells with blood and provides the right temperature for incubation. In most other species, the female develops the brood patch.

Other ID: white "eyebrow" and throat; light under-parts; black legs. *Nonbreeding:* all-grey upperparts; white "eyebrow"; grey "cap" and eye line; dark yellowish or greenish legs.
Size: *L* 22–24 cm; W 43 cm.
Voice: deep, grunting *work work* or *wu wu wu,* usually given on the breeding grounds.
Status: rare migrant and breeder.
Habitat: *Breeding:* cattail marshes and grass or sedge margins of sewage lagoons. *In migration:* lakeshores, marshes and sewage lagoons.

Similar Birds

Red-necked Phalarope

Red Phalarope

dark, needlelike bill

brown "cap" and eye line

black eye line extends down side of neck and onto back

pale chestnut sides of neck

grey "cap"

♂

chestnut brown sides of neck

♀

breeding

Nesting: often near water; well concealed in a depression lined with vegetation; brown-blotched, buff eggs are 37 x 24 mm; male incubates 4 eggs for 18–27 days and rears the young.

Did You Know?

A Phalarope female mates with several males. After laying eggs, she leaves her mate to incubate them and tend the young.

Look For

Unlike most birds, the female phalarope is more colourful than the male. The male phalarope's dull colours help camouflage him while he incubates the eggs.

Bonaparte's Gull
Larus philadelphia

This gull's jet-black head gives it an appealing elegance. With its delicate plumage and behaviour, the small Bonaparte's Gull is nothing like its brash relatives. It avoids landfills, preferring to dine on insects caught in midair or plucked from the water's surface. The Bonaparte's Gull only raises its soft, scratchy voice in excitement when it spies a school of fish or an intruder. • While other black-headed gulls in Ontario have orange bills, the Bonaparte's bill is black. The phrase "black-bill Bonaparte's" is a useful memory aid for identification.

Other ID: grey mantle; white underparts.
Nonbreeding: white head; dark ear patch.
In flight: white forewing wedge; black wing tips.
Size: *L* 30–36 cm; *W* 84 cm.
Voice: scratchy, soft *ear ear* while feeding.
Status: common to very common migrant in spring and autumn; uncommon breeder; rare to locally abundant winter visitor.
Habitat: *Breeding:* boreal forest. *In migration* and *winter:* large lakes, rivers and marshes.

Similar Birds

Franklin's Gull

Little Gull

Black-headed Gull

black head

black bill

nonbreeding

white eye ring

breeding

orange legs

Nesting: occasionally colonial; builds a shallow nest bowl on the short, thick branches of a conifer; brown-blotched, olive to buff eggs are 52 x 36 mm; pair incubates 3 eggs for 24 days.

Did You Know?

This gull was named after Charles-Lucien Bonaparte, a naturalist who made significant ornithological contributions in the 1800s.

Look For

From October to early December, Lake Erie and the Niagara River host huge flocks of Bonaparte's Gulls that can contain up to 100,000 birds.

Ring-billed Gull

Larus delawarensis

Few people can claim they have never seen this common and widespread gull. Highly tolerant of humans, Ring-billed Gulls are part of our everyday lives, scavenging our litter and fouling our vehicles. These omnivorous gulls will eat almost anything and they swarm parks, beaches, golf courses and fast-food parking lots looking for food handouts, causing some people to consider them pests. However, few species have adjusted to human development as well as the Ring-billed Gull, which is something to appreciate.

Other ID: pale grey mantle; white underparts. *In flight:* black wing tips with a few white spots.
Size: L 46–51 cm; W 1.2 m.
Voice: high-pitched *kakakaka-akakaka;* also a low, laughing *yook-yook-yook.*
Status: rare to locally very common migrant and winter visitor; uncommon to locally abundant breeder.
Habitat: *Breeding:* sparsely vegetated islands, open beaches, breakwaters and dredge-spoil areas. *In migration* and *winter:* lakes, rivers, landfills, golf courses, fields and parks.

Similar Birds

Herring Gull (p. 76) Glaucous Gull Thayer's Gull Iceland Gull

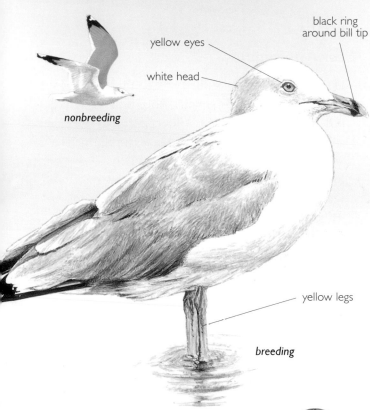

yellow eyes

black ring
around bill tip

white head

nonbreeding

yellow legs

breeding

Nesting: colonial; in a shallow scrape on the ground lined with grass, debris and sticks; brown-blotched, grey to olive eggs are 59 x 42 mm; pair incubates 2–4 eggs for 23–28 days.

Did You Know?

In chaotic nesting colonies, adult Ring-billed Gulls will call out and recognize the response of their chicks.

Look For

To differentiate between gulls, pay attention to the markings on their bills and the colour of their legs.

Herring Gull

Larus argentatus

Herring Gulls are as skilled at scrounging handouts on the beach as their smaller Ring-billed relatives, but Herring Gulls prefer wilderness areas over urban settings. They settle on lakes and large rivers where Ring-billed Gulls are not usually found. • A gull can stand on ice for hours without freezing its feet. The arteries and veins in its legs run close together, so that blood flowing to its extremities warms the cooler blood travelling back to its core.

Other ID: yellow bill; light eyes; light grey mantle; white underparts. *Nonbreeding:* white head and nape are washed with brown. *In flight:* white-spotted, black wing tips.
Size: L 58–66 cm; W 1.2 m.
Voice: loud, buglelike *kleew-kleew;* also an alarmed *kak-kak-kak.*
Status: abundant migrant; common to locally abundant breeder; locally abundant winter visitor.
Habitat: large lakes, wetlands, rivers, landfills and urban areas.

Similar Birds

Ring-billed Gull (p. 74)   Glaucous Gull   Thayer's Gull   Iceland Gull

nonbreeding

white head

red spot on
lower mandible

pink legs

breeding

Nesting: singly or colonially; on an open beach
or island; in a shallow scrape lined with vegetation
and sticks; darkly blotched, olive to buff eggs are
70 x 48 mm; pair incubates 3 eggs for 31–32 days.

Did You Know?

Though Herring Gulls are
skilled hunters, they are
opportunistic and scav-
enge on human leftovers
in fast-food parking lots
and landfills.

Look For

Nestlings use the small red
spot on the gull's lower bill
as a target. A hungry chick
will peck at the spot, cueing
the parent to regurgitate its
meal.

Common Tern
Sterna hirundo

Common Terns are sleek, agile birds. They patrol the shorelines of lakes and rivers during spring and fall, settling in large, noisy nesting colonies during the summer months. To win a mate, the male struts through the breeding colony with an offering of fish in his mouth. If a female accepts a suitor's gracious gift, they pair up to nest. Parents defend their nest by diving repeatedly and aggressively at intruders, and will even defecate on offenders to drive them away!

Other ID: white underparts and rump; white tail with grey outer edges. *Nonbreeding:* black nape; lacks black "cap." *In flight:* shallowly forked tail; long, pointed wings; dark grey wedge near lighter grey upperwing tips.
Size: *L* 33–41 cm; *W* 76 cm.
Voice: high-pitched, drawn-out *keee-are;* most commonly heard at colonies but also in foraging flights.
Status: common migrant and breeder; locally abundant in fall.
Habitat: large lakes, open wetlands, slow-moving rivers, islands and beaches.

Similar Birds

Forster's Tern

Arctic Tern (p. 78)

Caspian Tern

black "cap"

black tip on red bill

nonbreeding

red legs

breeding

Nesting: colonial; on an island; in a small scrape lined with pebbles, vegetation or shells; darkly blotched, creamy white eggs are 42 x 30 mm; pair incubates 1–3 eggs for 20–24 days.

Did You Know?

Terns are effortless fliers and impressive long-distance migrants. Once, a Common Tern banded in Great Britain was recovered in Australia.

Look For

Terns hover over the water, then dive headfirst to capture small fish or aquatic invertebrates below the surface.

Black Tern
Chlidonias niger

Black Terns rule the skies above cattail marshes. These acrobatic birds wheel about in feeding flights, picking minnows from the water's surface and catching insects in midair.
• Wetland habitat loss and degradation have caused Black Tern populations to decline. As well, these birds are sensitive nesters and will not return to a nesting area if the water level or plant density changes. Wetland conservation efforts may eventually help these birds recover to their former prosperity.

Other ID: *Breeding:* grey back, wings and tail; black bill. *Nonbreeding:* white underparts and forehead; molting fall birds may be mottled with brown. *In flight:* long, pointed wings; shallowly forked tail.
Size: *L* 23–25 cm; *W* 61 cm.
Voice: greeting call is a shrill, metallic *kik-kik-kik-kik-kik;* typical alarm call is *kreea.*
Status: locally uncommon to common migrant and breeder; a few may remain until mid-December.
Habitat: shallow, freshwater cattail marshes, wetlands, lake edges and sewage ponds with emergent vegetation.

Similar Birds

Forster's Tern

Common Tern (p. 78)

Caspian Tern

nonbreeding

black head
and underparts

white undertail
coverts

breeding

Nesting: loosely colonial; flimsy nest of dead plant material is built on floating vegetation, a muddy mound or a muskrat house; darkly blotched olive to pale buff eggs are 34 x 25 mm; pair incubates 3 eggs for 21–22 days.

Did You Know?

The Black Tern's genus name is a variation of *chelidonias*, the Greek word for "swallow." The name reflects the tern's darting, swallowlike flight pattern.

Look For

Flocks of Black Terns can be seen snatching insects from the air at dawn and dusk. They also gather to fly about just before and after a storm.

Rock Pigeon
Columba livia

The colourful and familiar Rock Pigeons have an unusual feature: they feed their young a substance similar to milk. These birds lack mammary glands, but they produce a nutritious liquid, called "pigeon milk," in their crops. A chick inserts its bill down the adult's throat to reach the thick, protein-rich fluid. • Rock Pigeons are likely the descendants of a Eurasian bird that was first domesticated about 4500 BC. Rock Pigeons have been used as pets and even as message couriers by the likes of Caesar and Napoleon.

Other ID: orange feet. *In flight:* holds wings in deep "V" while gliding.
Size: L 31–33 cm; W 71 cm (male is usually larger).
Voice: soft, cooing *coorrr-coorrr-coorrr*.
Status: locally abundant year-round resident.
Habitat: urban areas, railway yards and agricultural areas; high cliffs often provide more natural habitat.

Similar Birds

Mourning Dove (p. 84)

Look For

No other "wild" bird varies as much in coloration, a result of semi-domestication and extensive inbreeding over time.

colour is highly variable
(iridescent blue grey,
red, white or tan)

dark-tipped tail

Nesting: in a barn or on a cliff, bridge or tower; in a flimsy nest of sticks, grass and other vegetation; glossy white eggs are 39 × 29 mm; pair incubates 2 eggs for 16–19 days; may raise broods year-round.

Did You Know?

Rock Pigeons have also been used as scientific subjects. Much of our understanding of bird migration, endocrinology, sensory perception, flight, behaviour and other biological functions are derived from experiments involving Rock Pigeons.

Mourning Dove

Zenaida macroura

The Mourning Dove's soft cooing, which filters through broken woodlands and suburban parks, is often confused with the sound of a hooting owl. Curious birders who track down the source of the calls are often surprised to find the streamlined silhouette of a perched dove. • These popular game animals are some of the most abundant native birds in North America. Their numbers and range have increased since human development created more open habitats and food sources, such as waste grain and bird feeders.

Other ID: buffy, grey brown plumage; small head; dark bill; sleek body; dull red legs.
Size: *L* 28–33 cm; *W* 46 cm.
Voice: mournful, soft, slow *oh-woe-woe-woe*.
Status: abundant year-round resident; less common in the north; avoids heavily forested areas.
Habitat: open and riparian woodlands, forest edges, agricultural and suburban areas, open parks.

Similar Birds

Rock Pigeon (p. 82)

Yellow-billed Cuckoo

Black-billed Cuckoo

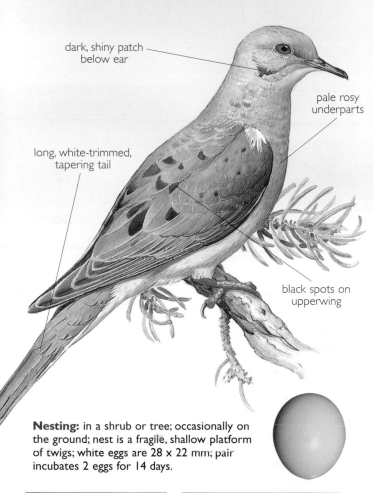

dark, shiny patch below ear

pale rosy underparts

long, white-trimmed, tapering tail

black spots on upperwing

Nesting: in a shrub or tree; occasionally on the ground; nest is a fragile, shallow platform of twigs; white eggs are 28 x 22 mm; pair incubates 2 eggs for 14 days.

Did You Know?

The Mourning Dove raises up to six broods each year—more than any other native bird.

Look For

When the Mourning Dove bursts into flight, its wings clap above and below its body. This bird also often creates a whistling sound when flying at a high speed.

Great Horned Owl
Bubo virginianus

This highly adaptable and superbly camouflaged hunter has sharp hearing and powerful vision that allow it to hunt at night as well as by day. It will swoop down from a perch onto almost any small creature that moves. • An owl has specially designed feathers on its wings: the leading edge of the first primary feather is serrated rather than smooth. This interrupts airflow over the wing and allows the owl to fly noiselessly. • Great Horned Owls begin their courtship as early as January, and by February and March, the females are already incubating their eggs.

Other ID: overall plumage varies from light grey to dark brown; heavily mottled grey, brown and black upperparts; yellow eyes; white "chin."
Size: L 46–64 cm; W 91–152 cm.
Voice: breeding call is 4–6 deep hoots: *hoo-hoo-hoooo hoo-hoo* or *Who's awake? Me too;* female gives higher-pitched hoots.
Status: fairly common year-round resident.
Habitat: fragmented forests, fields, riparian woodlands, suburban parks and wooded edges of landfills.

Similar Birds

Long-eared Owl

Great Gray Owl

Short-eared Owl

tall, widely spaced "ear" tufts form a triangle with beak

rusty orange facial disc is outlined in black

fine, horizontal barring on breast

Nesting: in a bird's abandoned stick nest or in a tree cavity; adds little or no nest material; dull whitish eggs are 56 x 47 mm; mostly the female incubates 2–3 eggs for 28–35 days.

Did You Know?

The Great Horned Owl has a poor sense of smell, which might explain why it is the only consistent predator of skunks.

Look For

Owls regurgitate pellets that contain the indigestible parts of their prey. You can find these pellets, which are generally clean and dry, under frequently used perches.

Snowy Owl

Bubo scandiacus

Feathered to the toes, the ghostly white Snowy Owl can remain active even in frigid winter temperatures. Its transparent plumage traps heat like a greenhouse. This bird also creates insulating air pockets between its body and the cold air by ruffling its feathers. • Snowy Owls are regular annual visitors in Ontario, but their numbers can fluctuate dramatically. When lemming and vole populations crash in the Arctic, large numbers of Snowy Owls venture south to search for food. • As Snowy Owls age, their plumage pales—older males are often pure white.

Other ID: *Male:* almost entirely white with very little dark flecking. *Female:* more dark flecking than male. *Immature:* heavier barring than adult female.
Size: *L* 51–69 cm; *W* 1.4–1.7 m (female is noticeably larger).
Voice: quiet during winter.
Status: irregular, very rare to uncommon winter visitor; very rare summer visitor and potential breeder.
Habitat: open country, including croplands, meadows and lakeshores; often perches on fence posts, buildings and utility poles.

Similar Birds

Northern Hawk Owl

Great Gray Owl

clean, white face

yellow eyes

black bill and talons

dark barring or flecking on breast and upperparts

♀

Nesting: nesting has not been confirmed in Ontario; glossy white eggs are 57 x 45 mm; female incubates 9–10 eggs for 32–33 days.

Did You Know?

The Snowy Owl may have inspired the first bird painting. Depictions of this bird have been found in prehistoric cave art.

Look For

An owl will often swoop down from its perch and punch through the snow to capture a rodent, leaving an imprint of its outstretched wings.

Northern Saw-whet Owl

Aegolius acadicus

The tiny Northern Saw-whet Owl makes the most of every hunting opportunity. When temperatures fall below freezing and prey is abundant, the Saw-whet will catch more than it can eat. It usually stores the extra food in trees and allows it to freeze. When hunting efforts fail, the hungry owl returns to thaw out the frozen cache, "incubating" the food as if it were a clutch of eggs! The Saw-whet's favourite foods include mice, voles, large insects and songbirds.

Other ID: large, rounded head; dark bill; short tail. *Juvenile:* white patch between eyes; rich brown head and breast; buff brown belly.
Size: *L* 18–23 cm; *W* 43–55 cm.
Voice: whistled, evenly spaced *whew-whew*, repeated about 100 times per minute.
Status: uncommon migrant in early spring and late autumn; rare to fairly common breeder; rare winter visitor.
Habitat: coniferous and mixed forests; wooded city parks and ravines.

Similar Birds

Boreal Owl

Eastern Screech-Owl

Northern Hawk Owl

pale, unbordered facial disc

white-streaked forehead

white-spotted, brown upperparts

vertical, rusty streaks on underparts

Nesting: in a natural tree hollow or a nest box; white eggs are 30 x 25 mm; female incubates 5–6 eggs for 27–29 days; male feeds the female during incubation.

Did You Know?

This owl's name refers to its call, which sounds like a saw blade being sharpened. It may remind you of the "bleeping" sound of a vehicle backing up.

Look For

In October, many of these owls gather on islands and peninsulas on the northern shores of Lake Erie and Lake Michigan.

Common Nighthawk
Chordeiles minor

The Common Nighthawk makes an unforgettable booming sound as it flies high overhead. In an energetic courting display, the male dives, then swerves skyward, making a hollow *vroom* sound with its wings. • Like other members of the nightjar family, the Common Nighthawk has adapted to catch insects in midair: its gaping mouth is surrounded by feather shafts that funnel insects into its beak. A nighthawk can eat over 2600 insects, including mosquitoes, blackflies and flying ants, in one day.

Other ID: *Female:* buff throat. *In flight:* bold, white "wrist" patches on long, pointed wings; shallowly forked, barred tail; erratic flight.
Size: *L* 22–25 cm; *W* 61 cm.
Voice: frequently repeated, nasal *peent peent;* wings make a deep, hollow *boom* during courtship dive.
Status: uncommon spring migrant and breeder; common to locally common fall migrant.
Habitat: *Breeding:* forest openings, burns, bogs, rocky outcroppings and gravel rooftops. *In migration:* often near water; any area with large numbers of flying insects.

Similar Birds

Chuck-will's-widow

Whip-poor-will

very small bill

white throat
on male

cryptic, mottled
plumage

♂

♂

barred underparts

Nesting: on bare ground; no nest is built; heavily
marked, creamy white to buff eggs are 30 x 22 mm;
female incubates 2 eggs for about 19 days; both
adults feed the young.

Did You Know?

It was once believed that
members of the nightjar,
or "goatsucker," family
could suck milk from the
udders of goats, causing
the goats to go blind!

Look For

With their short legs and
tiny feet, Nighthawks sit
lengthwise on tree branches
and blend in perfectly with
the bark.

Chimney Swift

Chaetura pelagica

Chimney Swifts are the "frequent fliers" of the bird world—they feed, drink, bathe, collect nesting material and even mate while they fly! They spend much of their time catching insects in the skies above Ontario's urban neighbourhoods. During night migrations, swifts sleep as they fly, relying on changing wind conditions to steer them.

• Chimney Swifts have small, weak legs and cannot take flight again if they land on the ground. For this reason, swifts usually cling to vertical surfaces with their strong claws.

Other ID: brown overall; slim body. *In flight:* rapid wingbeats; boomerang-shaped profile; erratic flight pattern.
Size: *L* 11–14 cm; *W* 30–23 cm.
Voice: call is a rapid *chitter-chitter-chitter,* given in flight; also gives a rapid series of staccato *chip* notes.
Status: common migrant in spring and fall; fairly common breeder.
Habitat: forages above cities and towns; roosts and nests in chimneys; may nest in tree cavities in more remote areas.

Similar Birds

Bank Swallow

Barn Swallow (p. 128)

Northern
Rough-winged Swallow

long, thin, pointed, crescent-shaped wings

squared tail

Nesting: often colonial; in a cavity, often a chimney; half-saucer nest of short, dead twigs is attached to a vertical wall; white eggs are 20 × 13 mm; pair incubates 4–5 eggs for 19–21 days.

Did You Know?

Migrating Chimney Swifts can fly at the same altitude as airplanes, approximately 3 km above the ground.

Look For

Swifts frequently nest in brick chimneys or abandoned buildings, and use saliva to attach their half-saucer nests to the walls.

Ruby-throated Hummingbird

Archilochus colubris

Ruby-throated Hummingbirds bridge the ecological gap between birds and bees—they feed on sweet, energy-rich flower nectar and pollinate the flowers in the process. Native, nectar-producing flowers such as honeysuckle or a sugarwater feeder can attract hummingbirds to your backyard. • Each year, Ruby-throated Hummingbirds migrate across the Gulf of Mexico—a nonstop, 800 km journey.

Other ID: iridescent, green back; pale underparts.
Immature: similar to female.
Size: *L* 9 cm; *W* 11 cm.
Voice: most noticeable is the soft buzzing of the wings while in flight; also produces a loud *chick* and other high squeaks.
Status: common migrant, especially in fall; uncommon breeder; a few may remain until mid-November.
Habitat: open, mixed woodlands, wetlands, orchards, tree-lined meadows, flower gardens and backyards with trees and feeders.

Similar Birds

Rufous Hummingbird

Look For

The hummingbird is among the few birds that can fly vertically and in reverse.

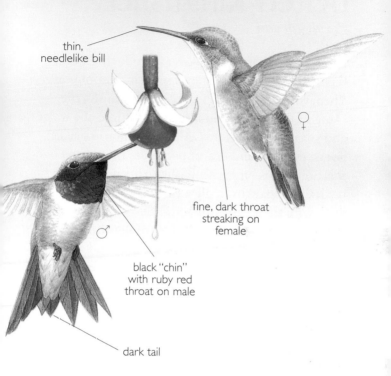

thin, needlelike bill

fine, dark throat streaking on female

black "chin" with ruby red throat on male

dark tail

Nesting: on a horizontal tree limb; tiny, deep cup nest of plant down and fibres is held together with spider silk; lichens and leaves are pasted on the exterior walls; white eggs are 13 x 8 mm; female incubates 2 eggs for 13–16 days.

Did You Know?

Weighing about as much as a nickel, a hummingbird can briefly reach speeds of up to 100 km per hour. In straight-ahead flight, hummingbirds beat their wings up to 80 times per second, and their hearts can beat up to 1200 times per minute!

Belted Kingfisher
Ceryle alcyon

Perched on a bare branch over a productive pool, the Belted Kingfisher utters a scratchy, rattling call. Then, with little regard for its scruffy hairdo, the "king of the fishers" plunges headfirst into the water and snags a fish or a frog. Many of Ontario's lakes, rivers, marshes and beaver ponds are monitored by this boisterous bird. • Kingfisher pairs nest on sandy banks, taking turns to dig a tunnel, up to 2 metres long, with their sturdy bills and claws. • In Greek mythology, Alcyon, the daughter of the wind god, grieved so deeply for her drowned husband that the gods transformed them both into kingfishers.

Other ID: bluish upperparts; long, small, white patch near eye; straight bill; short legs; white underwings.
Size: *L* 28–36 cm; *W* 51 cm.
Voice: fast, repetitive, cackling rattle, like a teacup shaking on a saucer.
Status: common migrant and breeder; rare winter visitor.
Habitat: rivers, large streams, lakes, marshes and beaver ponds, especially near exposed soil banks, gravel pits or bluffs.

Similar Birds

Blue Jay (p. 118)

Look For

These hardy birds don't hesitate to overwinter in the south of the province if there is open water available.

shaggy crest

white "collar"

♀

blue grey breast band

♂

rust-coloured "belt" on female may be incomplete

Nesting: in a cavity at the end of an earth burrow; glossy white eggs are 34 x 27 mm; pair incubates 6–7 eggs for 22–24 days; both adults feed the young.

Did You Know?

After a successful dive, the kingfisher flips its prey into the air and swallows it headfirst. Occasionally, prey is taken back to a perch where it is savagely pounded against an unyielding surface until stunned, and then gulped down.

Yellow-bellied Sapsucker
Sphyrapicus varius

Yellow-bellied Sapsuckers make their presence known in May, when the sounds of their knocking beaks echo throughout Ontario woodlands. Listen for pairs rapping in rhythmic duets. • Sapsuckers drill "wells" in tree trunks, which fill with sweet, sticky sap and attract insects. Yellow-bellied sapsuckers eat both the trapped bugs and pooled sap, and must defend the wells from other wildlife, including hummingbirds and small rodents.

Other ID: black-and-white face, back, wings and tail.
Male: red "chin." *Female:* white "chin."
Size: *L* 18–20 cm; *W* 41 cm.
Voice: nasal, catlike *meow;* territorial and courtship hammering has a distinctive 2-speed quality.
Status: uncommon to common migrant and breeder; a few may overwinter.
Habitat: deciduous and mixed forests, especially dry, second-growth woodlands.

Similar Birds

Red-headed
Woodpecker

Downy
Woodpecker (p. 102)

Hairy
Woodpecker

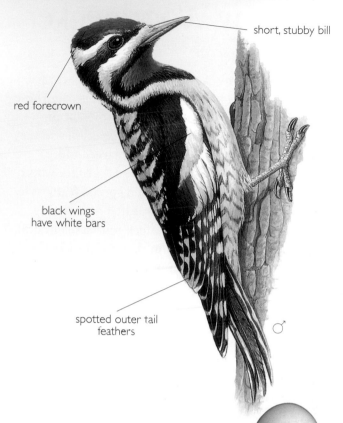

short, stubby bill

red forecrown

black wings
have white bars

spotted outer tail
feathers

♂

Nesting: a cavity lined with wood chips; usually in a live poplar or birch tree with heart rot; white eggs are 22 x 17 mm; pair incubates 5–6 eggs for 12–13 days.

Did You Know?

A sapsucker does not actually suck sap—it laps it up with a tongue that resembles a paintbrush.

Look For

Recently drilled wells arranged in parallel horizontal rows indicate that sapsuckers are nearby.

Downy Woodpecker
Picoides pubescens

A pair of Downy Woodpeckers at your backyard bird feeder will brighten a frosty winter day. These approachable little birds are more tolerant of human activities than most other species, and they visit feeders more often than the larger, more aggressive Hairy Woodpeckers. • Like other woodpeckers, the Downy has evolved special features to help cushion the shock of repeated hammering, including a strong bill and neck muscles, a flexible, reinforced skull and a brain that is tightly packed in its protective cranium.

Other ID: black eye line and crown; white belly. *Male:* small, red patch on back of head. *Female:* no red patch.
Size: *L* 15–18 cm; *W* 30 cm.
Voice: long, unbroken trill; calls are a sharp *pik* or *ki-ki-ki* or whiny *queek queek*.
Status: common year-round resident; rare in far northern Ontario.
Habitat: any wooded environment, especially deciduous and mixed forests and areas with tall, deciduous shrubs.

Similar Birds

Hairy Woodpecker

American Three-toed Woodpecker

Yellow-bellied Sapsucker (p. 100)

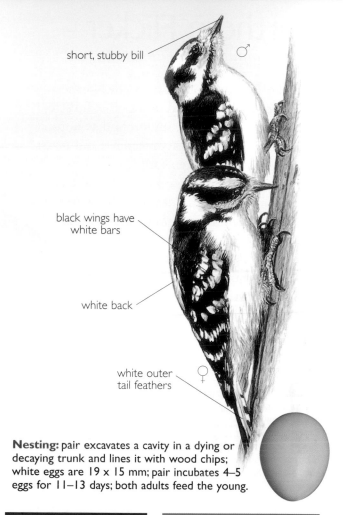

short, stubby bill ♂

black wings have
white bars

white back

white outer
tail feathers ♀

Nesting: pair excavates a cavity in a dying or decaying trunk and lines it with wood chips; white eggs are 19 x 15 mm; pair incubates 4–5 eggs for 11–13 days; both adults feed the young.

Did You Know?

Woodpeckers have feathered nostrils, which filter out the sawdust produced by hammering.

Look For

The Downy Woodpecker's stiff tail feathers help to prop up its body while it scales trees and excavates cavities.

Northern Flicker
Colaptes auratus

Instead of boring holes in trees, the Northern Flicker scours the ground in search of invertebrates, particularly ants. With robinlike hops, it investigates anthills, grassy meadows and forest clearings. • Flickers often bathe in dusty depressions. The dust particles absorb oils and bacteria that can harm the birds' feathers. To clean themselves even more thoroughly, flickers squash captured ants and preen themselves with the remains. Ants contain formic acid, which kills small parasites on the flickers' skin and feathers.

Other ID: long bill; brownish to buff face; grey crown; white rump. *Male:* black "moustache" stripe. *Female:* no "moustache."
Size: *L* 32–33 cm; *W* 51 cm.
Voice: loud, laughing, rapid *kick-kick-kick-kick-kick-kick; woika-woika-woika* issued during courtship.
Status: abundant migrant and breeder; rare to locally common in winter.
Habitat: open deciduous, mixed and coniferous woodlands and forest edges, fields, meadows, beaver ponds and other wetlands.

Similar Birds

Yellow-bellied
Sapsucker (p. 100)

Red-bellied
Woodpecker

barred, brown
back and wings

♂

buff to whitish
underparts

red nape crescent

black "bib"

♀

yellow underwings
and undertail

Nesting: pair excavates a cavity in a dying or decaying trunk and lines it with wood chips; may also use a nest box; white eggs are 28 x 22 mm; pair incubates 5–8 eggs for 11–16 days.

Did You Know?

The very long tongues of woodpeckers are stored in the skull in much the same way that a measuring tape is stored in its case.

Look For

Northern Flickers are partial to foraging at anthills and may visit their favourite colonies regularly, hammering and probing into the ground to unearth adults and larvae.

Pileated Woodpecker
Dryocopus pileatus

The Pileated Woodpecker, with its flaming red crest, chisel-like bill and commanding size, requires 40 hectares of mature forest as a home territory. Pairs settle in mature forests and spend up to six weeks excavating a large nest cavity in a dead or decaying tree. • A woodpecker's bill becomes shorter as the bird ages. In his historic painting of the Pileated Woodpecker, John J. Audubon correctly depicted the juvenile birds with slightly longer bills than the adults.

Other ID: predominantly black; yellow eyes; white "chin." *Male:* red "moustache." *Female:* no red "moustache"; grey brown forehead.
Size: L 41–48 cm; W 74 cm.
Voice: loud, fast, rolling *woika-woika-woika-woika;* long series of *kuk* notes; loud, resonant drumming.
Status: rare to uncommon year-round resident.
Habitat: extensive tracts of mature deciduous, mixed or coniferous forests; also riparian woodlands or woodlots in suburban and agricultural areas.

Similar Birds

Yellow-bellied
Sapsucker (p. 100)

Red-bellied
Woodpecker

Red-headed
Woodpecker

flaming red crest
extends farther
on male

stout,
dark bill

white stripe
runs from bill
to shoulder

white wing
linings

adult pair

Nesting: pair excavates a cavity in a dying or
decaying trunk and lines it with wood chips;
white eggs are 33 x 25 mm; pair incubates 4
eggs for 15–18 days; both adults feed the young.

Did You Know?

Ducks, small falcons, owls
and even flying squirrels
frequently nest in the
abandoned cavities of
Pileated Woodpeckers.

Look For

Pileated Woodpeckers leave
rectangular cavities and large
holes at the base of trees
while foraging.

Olive-sided Flycatcher

Contopus cooperi

The Olive-sided Flycatcher's upright, attentive posture contrasts with its comical song: *quick-three-beers! quick-three-beers!* Like a dutiful parent, this flycatcher changes its tune during nesting, when it more often produces an equally enthusiastic *pip-pip-pip.* • Olive-sided Flycatchers nest high in the forest canopy. Far above the forest floor, they have easy access to an abundance of flying insects, including honeybees and adult wood-boring and bark beetles.

Other ID: dark upper mandible; dull yellow orange lower mandible; inconspicuous eye ring; white tufts on sides of rump.

Size: *L* 18–20 cm; *W* 33 cm.

Voice: *Male:* song is a chipper and lively *quick-three-beers!,* with the second note highest in pitch; descending *pip-pip-pip* when excited.

Status: rare to fairly common migrant; uncommon to locally common breeder.

Habitat: semi-open mixed and coniferous forests near water; prefers burned areas and wetlands.

Similar Birds

Eastern Wood-Pewee

Eastern Kingbird (p. 110)

Eastern Phoebe

olive grey to olive brown upperparts

light throat and belly

dark, olive grey "vest"

Nesting: high in a conifer, usually on a branch far from the trunk; nest of twigs and plant fibres is bound with spider silk; darkly spotted, white to pinkish buff eggs are 22 × 16 mm; female incubates 3 eggs for 14–17 days.

Did You Know?

Olive-sided Flycatchers are fierce nest defenders and will harass and chase off squirrels and other predators.

Look For

A big-headed silhouette on the tip of a mature conifer or dead branch may well belong to this feisty flycatcher.

Eastern Kingbird
Tyrannus tyrannus

The Eastern Kingbird fearlessly attacks crows, hawks and even humans that pass through its territory, pursuing and pecking at them until it feels the threat has passed. No one familiar with the Eastern Kingbird's pugnacious behaviour will refute its scientific name, *Tyrannus tyrannus.* • Eastern Kingbirds are common and widespread. On a drive in the country you will likely spot at least one of these birds sitting on a fence or utility wire. • This bird eats over 200 kinds of insects and will hover above shrubs or trees to pick berries, especially sassafras.

Other ID: no eye ring; black legs.
Size: *L* 22 cm; *W* 38 cm.
Voice: call is a quick, loud, chattering *kit-kit-kitter-kitter;* also a *buzzy dzee-dzee-dzee.*
Status: common to very common migrant and breeder.
Habitat: rural fields with scattered trees or hedgerows, clearings in fragmented forests, open roadsides, burned areas and near human settlements.

Similar Birds

Olive-sided
Flycatcher (p. 106)

Eastern
Wood-Pewee

Western Kingbird

small head crest

thin orange red crown
(rarely seen)

dark grey to black
upperparts

black bill

white underparts

white-tipped tail

Nesting: on a horizontal limb, stump or upturned tree root; cup nest is made of weeds, twigs and grass; darkly blotched, white to pinkish white eggs are 24 x 18 mm; female incubates 3–4 eggs for 14–18 days.

Did You Know?

Eastern Kingbirds rarely walk or hop on the ground—they prefer to fly, even for very short distances.

Look For

The Eastern Kingbird reveals its gentler side in a quivering, butterflylike courtship flight.

Northern Shrike
Lanius excubitor

As one of the most vicious predators, and considered the only true carnivorous bird, the Northern Shrike relies on its sharp, hooked bill to catch and kill small birds or rodents. They hunt from treetop perches and have a tendency to impale prey on thorns and barbs for later consumption. This habit has earned it the "Butcher Bird." • Northern Shrikes visit southern Ontario each winter in unpredictable and highly variable numbers. Africa and Eurasia are thought to have the greatest diversity of shrike species.

Other ID: black tail and wings; finely barred, pale underparts; pale grey upperparts. *In flight:* white wing patches.
Size: L 25 cm; W 37 cm.
Voice: usually silent; occasionally gives a long grating laugh: *raa-raa-raa-raa*.
Status: uncommon to erratic migrant and winter visitor; rare breeder.
Habitat: open country, including fields, shrubby areas, forest clearings and roadsides.

Similar Birds

Loggerhead Shrike

Northern Mockingbird

black "mask" does not extend above hooked bill

white outer tail feathers

pale lower mandible

Nesting: on the taiga in a spruce, willow or shrub; bulky nest is made of sticks, bark and moss; greenish white to buff eggs with reddish brown spotting are 29 x 19 mm; female incubates 4–7 eggs for 15–17 days.

Did You Know?

Shrikes possess extremely acute vision. One shrike spotted flying bumblebees at least 90 m away!

Look For

You might spot this bird taking advantage of a group of distracted songbirds at winter feeding stations.

Red-eyed Vireo
Vireo olivaceus

The male Red-eyed Vireo can out-sing any one of his courting neighbours. Capable of delivering about 40 phrases per minute, one tenacious male set a record by singing 21,000 in one day! Though you may still hear the Red-eyed Vireo singing five or six hours after other songbirds have ceased for the day, this bird conceals itself well in its olive brown plumage amongst the foliage of deciduous trees. Its unique red eyes, unusual among song-birds, are even trickier to spot without a good pair of binoculars.

Other ID: black-bordered, olive "cheek"; olive green upperparts.
Size: *L* 15 cm; *W* 24 cm.
Voice: call is a short, scolding *neeah. Male:* song is a series of quick, continuous, vari-able phrases with pauses in between: *look-up, way-up, tree-top, see-me, here-I-am!*
Status: very common migrant and breeder in spring and summer; occa-sionally remains until November.
Habitat: deciduous woodlands with a shrubby understorey.

Similar Birds

Philadelphia Vireo

Tennessee Warbler

Warbling Vireo

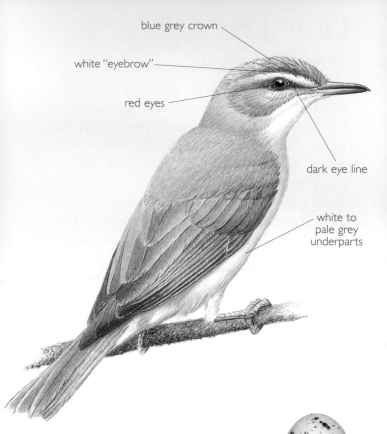

blue grey crown

white "eyebrow"

red eyes

dark eye line

white to pale grey underparts

Nesting: in a tree or shrub; hanging cup nest is made of grass, roots, spider silk and cocoons; darkly spotted, white eggs are 20 x 14 mm; female incubates 4 eggs for 11–14 days.

Did You Know?

These vireos are parasitized by Brown-headed Cowbirds and either abandon their nests or raise the cowbird young with their own.

Look For

The Red-eyed Vireo perches with a hunched stance and hops with its body turned diagonally to its direction of travel.

Gray Jay
Perisoreus canadensis

The friendly, mischievous Gray Jay sports a dark grey cloak and a long, elegant tail. These bold birds form strong pair bonds, and after an absence, partners will seek each other out and touch or nibble bills. • Gray Jays lay their eggs and begin incubation as early as late February, allowing the young to get a head start on learning to forage and store food. These birds cache food for the winter. Their specialized salivary glands coat the food with a sticky mucus that helps to preserve it.

Other ID: dark bill; white forehead, "cheek" and throat; white undertail coverts.
Size: *L* 28–33 cm; *W* 45 cm.
Voice: calls include a soft, whistled *quee-oo,* a chuckled *cla-cla-cla* and a *churr,* also imitates other birds.
Status: common year-round resident.
Habitat: dense and open coniferous and mixed forests, bogs and fens; picnic sites and campgrounds.

Similar Birds

Northern Shrike (p. 112)

Northern Mockingbird

Loggerhead Shrike

dark grey nape and upperparts

fluffy, pale grey breast and belly

long tail

Nesting: in a conifer; insulated nest of plant fibres, roots, moss, twigs, feathers and fur; speckled, pale grey to greenish eggs are 29 x 21 mm; female incubates 3–4 eggs for 17–22 days.

Did You Know?

The nickname "Whiskey Jack" is derived from the Algonquin name for this bird, *wis-kat-jon;* other names include "Canada Jay" and "Camp Robber."

Look For

Gray Jays are most often found in the campgrounds and picnic areas of Ontario's northern Shield country.

Blue Jay
Cyanocitta cristata

In Ontario, the Blue Jay is the only member of the corvid family dressed in blue. It is easily recognizable with its white-flecked wing feathers and sharply defined facial features. This major league mascot can be quite aggressive when competing for sunflower seeds and peanuts at backyard feeding stations, and it rarely hesitates to drive away smaller birds, squirrels or even cats when it feels threatened. Even the Great Horned Owl is not too formidable a predator for a group of these brave, boisterous mobsters to harass.

Other ID: blue upperparts; white underparts; black bill.
Size: *L* 28–31 cm; *W* 40 cm.
Voice: noisy, screaming *jay-jay-jay;* nasal *queedle queedle queedle-queedle* sounds like a muted trumpet; often imitates various sounds, including calls of other birds.
Status: common to abundant migrant and breeder; uncommon to fairly common visitor in winter.
Habitat: mixed deciduous forests, agricultural areas, scrubby fields and townsites.

Similar Birds

Eastern Bluebird (p. 140)

Belted Kingfisher (p. 98)

blue crest

white bars
and flecking
on wings

black "necklace"

dark bars and
white corners
on blue tail

Nesting: in a tree or tall shrub; pair builds a
bulky stick nest; greenish, buff or pale grey eggs,
spotted with olive and brown, are 28 x 20 mm;
pair incubates 4–5 eggs for 16–18 days.

Did You Know?

Blue Jays store food col-
lected at feeders in trees
and other discreet places
for later consumption.

Look For

The Blue Jay is an abundant,
adaptable bird present in
Ontario from March to
November and commonly
visits the south of the
province in winter.

American Crow
Corvus brachyrhynchos

The noise that emanates from this treetop squawker seems not to be representative of its intelligence. However, these wary, clever birds are impressive mimics, able to whine like a dog and laugh or cry like a human. • Crows are family-oriented, and the young from the previous year help their parents to raise the next year's nestlings. • American Crows are ecological generalists, able to adapt to a variety of habitats. They are common throughout the province in summer, but generally congregate in the extreme south of Ontario or migrate to the U.S. for winter.

Other ID: glossy, purple black plumage; black bill and legs.
Size: *L* 43–53 cm; *W* 94 cm.
Voice: distinctive, far-carrying, repetitive *caw-caw-caw*.
Status: common to abundant migrant and breeder in spring, summer and fall; common to locally abundant winter visitor.
Habitat: urban areas, agricultural fields and other open areas with scattered woodlands, marshes, lakes and rivers in densely forested areas.

Similar Birds

Common Raven (p. 122)

Black-billed Magpie

slim, sleek head and throat

square-shaped tail

Nesting: in a coniferous or deciduous tree or on a utility pole; large stick-and-branch nest is lined with fur and soft plant materials; darkly blotched, grey green to blue green eggs are 41 x 29 mm; female incubates 4–6 eggs for about 18 days.

Did You Know?

American Crows group together in fall in large flocks known as "murders."

Look For

Look for the square tail and slimmer bill of the American Crow and the wedge-shaped tail and heavier bill of the Common Raven to distinguish these similar birds.

Common Raven
Corvus corax

The Common Raven soars with a wingspan comparable to that of a hawk's, travelling along coastlines, over deserts, along mountain ridges and even on the arctic tundra. Few birds occupy such a large natural range. • Ravens have complex vocalizations and have even been spotted sliding down snowbanks. • Like crows, ravens are intelligent members of the corvid family and they maintain loyal, lifelong pair bonds.

Other ID: all-black plumage; rounded wings.
Size: *L* 61 cm; *W* 1.3 m.
Voice: deep, guttural, far-carrying, repetitive *craww-craww* or *quork quork* among other vocalizations.
Status: uncommon to common year-round resident.
Habitat: coniferous and mixed forests and woodlands; townsites, campgrounds and landfills.

Similar Birds

American Crow (p. 120)

Look For

When working as a pair to confiscate a meal, one raven may act as the decoy while the other steals the food.

heavy,
black bill

shaggy throat

wedge-shaped tail

Nesting: on a ledge, bluff or utility pole or in a tall coniferous tree; large stick and-branch nest is lined with fur and soft plant materials; variably marked, greenish eggs are 50 x 33 mm; female incubates 4–6 eggs for 18–21 days.

Did You Know?

The Common Raven, capable of living up to 40 years, once inhabited every corner of Ontario, but poisoning, trapping and shooting campaigns in the past led to great declines in their population.

Horned Lark
Eremophila alpestris

An impressive, high-speed, plummeting courtship dive would blow anybody's hair back, or in the case of the Horned Lark, its two unique black horns. Long before the snow is gone, this bird's tinkling song is one of the first introductions to spring.
• Horned Larks are often abundant at roadsides, searching for seeds, but an approaching vehicle usually sends them flying into an adjacent field, making them difficult to identify. When these birds visit in winter, you can spot them in farmers' fields or catch them at the beach visiting with Snow Buntings and Lapland Longspurs.

Other ID: *Male:* pale throat; dull brown upperparts. *Female:* duller plumage.
Size: *L* 18 cm; *W* 30 cm.
Voice: call is a tinkling *tsee-titi* or *zoot;* flight song is a long series of tinkling, twittered whistles.
Status: common migrant and breeder; rare to locally common visitor in winter.
Habitat: *Breeding:* open areas, including pastures, croplands, airfields and alpine tundra. *In migration* and *winter:* croplands, roadside ditches and fields.

Similar Birds

Snow Bunting

Lapland Longspur

American Pipit

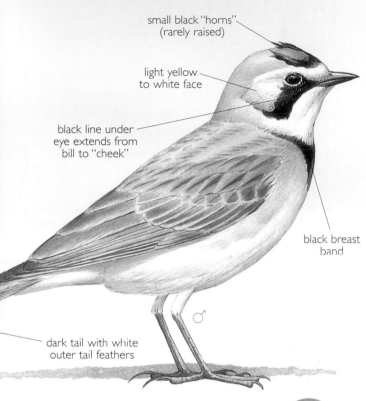

small black "horns" (rarely raised)

light yellow to white face

black line under eye extends from bill to "cheek"

black breast band

dark tail with white outer tail feathers

♂

Nesting: on the ground; in a shallow scrape lined with grass, plant fibres and roots; brown-blotched, grey to greenish white eggs are 23 x 16 mm; female incubates 3–4 eggs for 10–12 days.

Did You Know?

One way to distinguish a sparrow from a Horned Lark is by its method of travel: Horned Larks walk, whereas sparrows hop.

Look For

The Horned Lark's dark tail contrasts with its light brown body and belly. Field marks will help you to spot these birds in open-country habitat.

Purple Martin
Progne subis

In return for you setting up luxurious "condo complexes" for these large swallows, they will entertain you throughout spring and summer. Martin adults spiral around their accommodations in pursuit of flying insects, while their young perch clumsily at the cavity openings. Purple Martins once nested in natural tree hollows and in cliff crevices, but now have virtually abandoned these in favour of human-made housing. • To avoid the invasion of aggressive House Sparrows or European Starlings, it is essential for martin condos to be cleaned out and closed up after each nesting season.

Other ID: pointed wings; small bill.
Female: sooty grey underparts.
Size: *L* 18–20 cm; *W* 45 cm.
Voice: rich, fluty, robinlike *pew-pew,* often heard in flight.
Status: locally common migrant and breeder in spring and summer; a few remain until late October.
Habitat: semi-open areas, often near water.

Similar Birds

European Starling (p. 146)

Barn Swallow (p. 128)

Tree Swallow

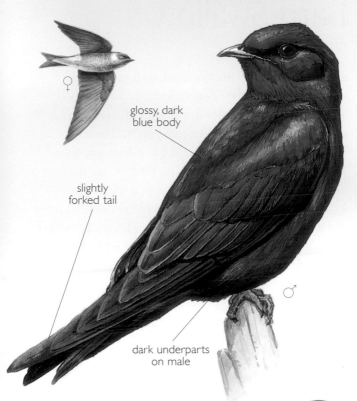

glossy, dark
blue body

slightly
forked tail

♀

♂

dark underparts
on male

Nesting: communal; in a human-made birdhouse, a hollowed-out gourd; nest is made of feathers, grass and mud; white eggs are 24 x 17 mm; female incubates 4–5 eggs for 15–18 days.

Did You Know?

The Purple Martin is North America's largest swallow.

Look For

You will have better success attracting Purple Martins to your martin condo complex if it is erected in an open area, high on a pole and near a body of water.

Barn Swallow
Hirundo rustica

In an encounter with this bird, you might first notice its distinctive, deeply forked tail—or you might just find yourself repeatedly ducking to avoid the dives of a protective parent. Barn Swallows once nested on cliffs, but they are now found more frequently nesting on human-made structures. Barns, boathouses and areas under bridges and house eaves all provide shelter from predators and inclement weather. The messy young and aggressive parents unfortunately often bring people to remove nests just as nesting season is beginning, but this bird's close association with humans allows us to observe the normally secretive reproductive cycle of birds.

Other ID: blue black upperparts; long, pointed wings.
Size: *L* 18 cm; *W* 38 cm.
Voice: continuous, twittering chatter: *zip-zip-zip* or *kvick-kvick*.
Status: common to abundant migrant and breeder; some remain until January.
Habitat: open rural and urban areas where human-made structures are near water.

Similar Birds

Cliff Swallow

Purple Martin (p. 126)

Tree Swallow

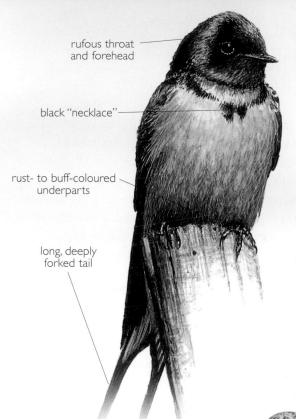

rufous throat
and forehead

black "necklace"

rust- to buff-coloured
underparts

long, deeply
forked tail

Nesting: singly or in small, loose colonies; on a human-made structure under an overhang; half or full cup nest is made of mud, grass and straw; brown-spotted, white eggs are 20 x 14 mm; pair incubates 4–7 eggs for 13–17 days.

Did You Know?

The Barn Swallow is a natural pest controller, feeding on insects that are often harmful to crops and livestock.

Look For

Barn Swallows roll mud into small balls and build their nests one mouthful of mud at a time.

Black-capped Chickadee
Poecile atricapillus

You can catch a glimpse of this incredibly sociable chickadee at any time of the year in Ontario. In winter, Black-caps join the company of kinglets, nuthatches, creepers and small woodpeckers to feed; in spring and fall, they join mixed flocks of vireos and warblers. While observing their antics at feeders, you may even be able to entice a Black-capped Chickadee to the palm of your hand with the help of a sunflower seed. • On cold nights, chickadees enter into a hypothermic state, lowering their body temperature and heartbeat considerably to conserve energy.

Other ID: black "bib"; white underparts; light buff sides and flanks; dark legs.
Size: *L* 13–15 cm; *W* 20 cm.
Voice: call is a chipper, whistled *chick-a-dee-dee-dee;* song is a slow, whistled *swee-tee* or *fee-bee.*
Status: common year-round resident.
Habitat: deciduous and mixed forests, riparian woodlands, wooded urban parks, backyard feeders.

Similar Birds

Carolina Chickadee

Boreal Chickadee

Blackpoll Warbler

black "cap"

white "cheek"

grey back
and wings

white edging on
wing feathers

Nesting: pair excavates a cavity in a rotting tree
or stump; cavity is lined with fur, feathers, moss,
grass and cocoons; occasionally uses a birdhouse;
finely speckled, white eggs are 15 x 12 mm;
female incubates 6–8 eggs for 12–13 days.

Did You Know?

Black-capped Chickadees
are thought to possess
amazing memories. They
can relocate seed caches
up to a month after they
are hidden!

Look For

The Black-capped Chickadee
sometimes feeds while hanging upside down, giving it the
chance to grab a treat
another bird may not be
able to reach.

Red-breasted Nuthatch
Sitta canadensis

The Red-breasted Nuthatch may look a little like a woodpecker, but its view of the world could be considered somewhat dizzying. This interesting bird, with its distinctive black eye line and red breast, moves down tree trunks headfirst, cleaning up the seeds, insects and nuts that woodpeckers may have overlooked. • The odd name "nuthatch" comes from this bird's habit of wedging large nuts into crevices, then using its bill to hammer the nuts open. • This bird's species name, *canadensis,* means "of Canada."

Other ID: white "cheek"; straight bill; short tail. *Male:* black crown. *Female:* dark grey crown.
Size: *L* 11 cm; *W* 21 cm.
Voice: call is a slow, repeated, nasal *yank yank yank;* also a short *tsip.*
Status: rare to fairly common year-round resident.
Habitat: *Breeding:* spruce–fir and pine forests; pine plantations. *In migration* and *winter:* mixed woodlands, especially those near bird feeders.

Similar Birds

White-breasted
Nuthatch

Look For

The Red-breasted Nuthatch visits feeders, but you may only catch a glimpse of its red belly as it grabs a seed and darts away to eat it in private.

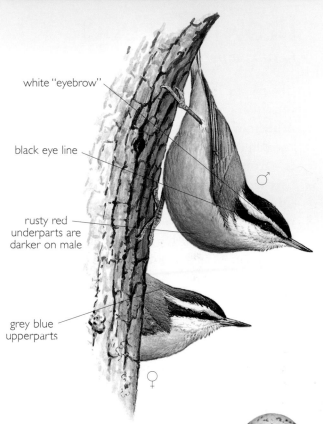

white "eyebrow"

black eye line

rusty red underparts are darker on male

grey blue upperparts

♂

♀

Nesting: excavates a cavity or uses an abandoned woodpecker nest; nest is made of bark shreds, grass and fur with sap spread at entrance; brown-spotted white eggs are 15 x 12 mm; female incubates 5–6 eggs for about 12 days.

Did You Know?

Red-breasted Nuthatches smear the entrance of their nest cavities with sap from pine and spruce trees to keep ants and other insects away; these creatures can transmit fungal infections or parasitize nestlings.

Brown Creeper
Certhia americana

The cryptic Brown Creeper is never easy to find, often going unnoticed until a flake of bark suddenly moves and takes the shape of a bird. A frightened creeper will freeze and flatten itself against a tree trunk, becoming nearly invisible. • The Brown Creeper uses its long, stiff tail feathers to prop itself up while climbing vertical tree trunks. When it reaches the upper branches, it floats down to the base of a neighbouring tree to begin another foraging ascent. As well as eating caterpillars and spiders, the Brown Creeper also visits suet feeders.

Other ID: brown upperparts with buffy white streaks; white underparts; rufous rump.
Size: *L* 13 cm; *W* 19 cm.
Voice: song is a faint, high-pitched *trees-trees-trees see the trees;* call is a high *tseee.*
Status: common migrant; uncommon breeder; rare winter visitor.
Habitat: mature deciduous, coniferous and mixed forests and woodlands, especially in wet areas with large, dead trees; also found near bogs.

Similar Birds

Common Nighthawk
(p. 92)

Red-breasted
Nuthatch (p. 132)

Northern Flicker
(p. 104)

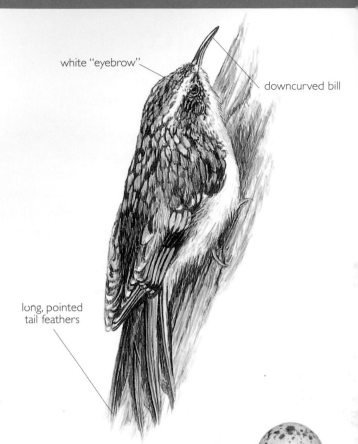

white "eyebrow"

downcurved bill

long, pointed
tail feathers

Nesting: under loose bark; nest of grass and
conifer needles is woven together with spider
silk; brown-spotted, whitish eggs are 15 x 12 mm;
female incubates 5–6 eggs for 14–17 days.

Did You Know?

There are many species
of creepers in Europe and
Asia, but the Brown
Creeper is the only mem-
ber of its family found in
North America.

Look For

The Brown Creeper feeds
by slowly spiraling up a tree
trunk, searching for hidden
invertebrates.

House Wren
Troglodytes aedon

You might overlook the bland, nondescript plumage of this suburban and city park dweller when you hear it sing a seemingly unending song in one breath. The voice of a House Wren is as sweet as that of a nightingale. • Despite their bubbly warble, House Wrens can be very aggressive toward other species that nest in their territory. They will even puncture and toss eggs from other birds' nests. • House Wrens often build numerous nests, which later serve as decoys or "dummy" nests to fool would-be enemies.

Other ID: whitish throat; brown upperparts; whitish to buff underparts; faintly barred flanks.
Size: *L* 12 cm; *W* 15 cm.
Voice: smooth, running, bubbly warble: *tsi-tsi-tsi-tsi oodle-oodle-oodle-oodle.*
Status: common migrant and breeder; a few may be present in winter.
Habitat: thickets and shrubby openings in or at the edge of deciduous or mixed woodlands; often in shrubs and thickets near buildings.

Similar Birds

Winter Wren

Sedge Wren

upraised tail

fine, dark barring on
upper wings and
lower back

faint, pale "eyebrow"
and eye ring

Nesting: in a natural or artificial cavity or abandoned woodpecker nest; nest of sticks and grass lined with feathers and fur; heavily marked, white to pinkish white eggs are 16 x 13 mm; female incubates 6–8 eggs for 12–15 days.

Did You Know?

This bird has the largest range of any New World passerine, stretching from Canada to southern South America.

Look For

The House Wren usually carries its short, finely barred tail pointing upward.

Ruby-crowned Kinglet
Regulus calendula

Not only does the male Ruby-crowned Kinglet possess a loud, complex, warbling song to bring him some attention, he also wears a nifty red "mohawk" to help attract a mate and defend his territory in spring. This kinglet's familiar voice echoes through Ontario's boreal forest in May and June. Unfortunately, the distinctive crown of the Ruby-crowned Kinglet is only visible in breeding season, leaving the bird to wear its dull olive green plumage for the rest of the year.

Other ID: olive green upperparts; dark wings; whitish to yellowish underparts; flicks its wings. *Female:* lacks red crown.
Size: *L* 10 cm; *W* 19 cm.
Voice: *Male:* song is an accelerating and rising *tea-tea-tea-tew-tew-tew look-at-me, look-at-me, look-at-me.*
Status: common to abundant migrant; uncommon to very common breeder; rare winter visitor.
Habitat: mixed woodlands and pure coniferous forests, especially with spruce; often near wet forest openings and edges.

Similar Birds

Golden-crowned Kinglet

Orange-crowned Warbler

Yellow-bellied Flycatcher

2 white wing bars

♀

male's small, red crown
is usually hidden

short, dark tail

bold, broken
eye ring

♂

Nesting: usually in a conifer; female builds
hanging nest of lichen, twigs and leaves; brown-
spotted, white to pale buff eggs are 14 x 11 mm;
female incubates 7–8 eggs for 13–14 days.

Did You Know?

Females can lay an
impressively large clutch
with up to 12 eggs, which
together often weigh as
much as the bird!

Look For

Watch for this bird's hovering
technique and wing-flicking
behaviour to distinguish it
from similar-looking flycatcher
species.

Eastern Bluebird

...alia sialis

The Eastern Bluebird's enticing colours are like those of a warm setting sun against a deep blue sky. This cavity nester's survival has been put to the test in the past—populations have declined in the presence of the competitive, introduced House Sparrow and European Starling. The removal of standing dead trees has also diminished nest site availability. Thankfully, bluebird enthusiasts and organizations have developed "bluebird trails" and mounted nest boxes on fence posts along highways and rural roads, allowing Eastern Bluebird numbers to gradually recover.

Other ID: dark bill; dark legs. *Female:* thin, white eye ring; grey brown head and back tinged with blue; blue wings and tail; paler chestnut underparts.
Size: *L* 18 cm; *W* 33 cm.
Voice: song is a rich, warbling *turr, turr-lee, turr-lee;* call is a chittering *pew.*
Status: uncommon migrant and breeder; rare winter visitor.
Habitat: cropland fencelines, meadows, fallow and abandoned fields, pastures, forest clearings and edges, golf courses, large lawns and cemeteries.

Similar Birds

Mountain Bluebird

Indigo Bunting (p. 166)

deep blue
upperparts

chestnut red
"chin," throat
and sides

white belly and
undertail coverts

♂

Nesting: in a natural cavity or nest box; female
builds a cup nest of grass, weed stems and small
twigs; pale blue eggs are 21 x 16 mm; female
incubates 4–5 eggs for 13–16 days.

Did You Know?

A cold spell in spring can
kill the Eastern Bluebird,
freezing the eggs and the
adult while it sits on the
nest.

Look For

Building a bluebird nest box
is a good winter project. The
birdhouse should have an
entrance that is perfect for a
bluebird, but small enough to
keep out competitors.

American Robin
Turdus migratorius

Come March, the familiar song of the American Robin may wake you early if you are a light sleeper. This abundant bird adapts easily to urban areas and often works from dawn until after dusk when there is a nest to be built or hungry, young mouths to feed. • The robin's bright red belly contrasted with its dark head and wings make the robin easy to identify even for a nonbirder. • Fermenting fruit on trees may convince these birds to stay for winter in the south of the province, where they gather in roosts to drink the intoxicating juices.

Other ID: incomplete, white eye ring; grey brown back; white undertail coverts.
Size: *L* 25 cm; *W* 43 cm.
Voice: song is an evenly spaced warble: *cheerily cheer-up cheerio;* call is a rapid *tut-tut-tut.*
Status: abundant migrant and breeder; rare to uncommon winter resident.
Habitat: residential lawns and gardens, pastures, urban parks, broken forests, bogs and river shorelines.

Similar Birds

Varied Thrush

Look For

A hunting robin with its head tilted to the side isn't listening for prey—it is actually looking for movements in the soil, waiting for its next meal to surface.

black head

white throat is streaked with black

dark grey head

black-tipped, yellow bill

brick red breast is darker on male

♂ ♀

Nesting: in a coniferous or deciduous tree or shrub; cup nest is built of grass, moss, bark and mud; light blue eggs are 28 x 20 mm; female incubates 4 eggs for 11–16 days.

Did You Know?

American Robins do not use nest boxes, but prefer platforms for their nests. The female stays busy raising up to three broods per year, and her young are easily distinguishable with their dishevelled plumage and heavily spotted underparts.

Gray Catbird

Dumetella carolinensis

This accomplished mimic may have you fooled if you should hear it shuffling through underbrush and dense riparian shrubs, calling its catlike *meow*. The Gray Catbird's ability to use both sides of its syrinx allows it to sing two notes at once. • In a competitive nesting habitat of sparrows, robins and cowbirds, the Gray Catbird vigilantly defends its territory. It will destroy the eggs and nestlings of other songbirds and take on an intense defensive posture, screaming and even attempting to hit an intruder when approached.

Other ID: dark grey overall; black eyes, bill and legs.
Size: *L* 11–14 cm; *W* 28 cm.
Voice: calls include a catlike *meoww* and a harsh *check-check;* song is a variety of warbles, squeaks and mimicked phrases interspersed with a *mew* call.
Status: uncommon to common migrant and breeder; a few may linger in winter.
Habitat: dense thickets, brambles, shrubby or brushy areas and hedgerows, often near water.

Similar Birds

Northern
Mockingbird

Gray Jay (p. 116)

Townsend's
Solitaire

black "cap"

long tail is dark
grey to black

chestnut
undertail coverts

Nesting: in a dense shrub or thicket; bulky cup nest is made of twigs, leaves and grass; greenish blue eggs are 23 x 17 mm; female incubates 4 eggs for 12–15 days.

Did You Know?

The watchful female Gray Catbird can recognize a Brown-headed Cowbird egg and will remove it from her nest.

Look For

If you are lucky enough to catch a glimpse of this bird during breeding season, watch the male raise his long tail to show off his chestnut-coloured undertail coverts.

European Starling
Sturnus vulgaris

The European Starling did not hesitate to make itself known across North America after being released in New York's Central Park in 1890 and 1891. These highly adaptable birds not only took over the nesting sites of native cavity nesters, such as Tree Swallows and Red-headed Woodpeckers, but they learned to mimic the sounds of Killdeers, Red-tailed Hawks, Soras and meadowlarks. European Starlings are now the most common bird in areas of southern Ontario. • Look for these birds in massive evening roosts under bridges or on buildings. • European Starlings have a variable diet consisting of Japanese beetles and other destructive agricultural pests, berries, grains and even human food waste.

Other ID: dark eyes; iridescent black breast; short, squared tail. *Nonbreeding:* feather tips are heavily spotted with white and buff.
Size: *L* 22 cm; *W* 40 cm.
Voice: variety of whistles, squeaks and gurgles; imitates other birds.
Status: abundant year-round resident.
Habitat: agricultural areas, townsites, woodland edges, landfills and roadsides.

Similar Birds

Rusty Blackbird

Brown-headed Cowbird (p. 174)

Brewer's Blackbird

iridescent, purple black head and neck

glossy, green back with buffy spots

yellow bill

greenish black underparts

breeding

Nesting: in an abandoned woodpecker cavity, natural cavity or nest box; nest is made of grass, twigs and straw; bluish to greenish white eggs are 30 × 21 mm; female incubates 4–6 eggs for 12–14 days.

Did You Know?

This bird was brought to New York as part of the Shakespeare society's plan to introduce all the birds mentioned in their favourite author's writings.

Look For

The European Starling looks somewhat like a blackbird. Look for the starling's comparably shorter tail and bright yellow bill to help you accurately identify it.

Cedar Waxwing
Bombycilla cedrorum

With its black "mask" and slick hairdo, the Cedar Waxwing has a heroic look. The splendid personality of this bird is reflected in its amusing antics after it gorges on fermented berries and in its gentle courtship dance. To court a mate, the gentlemanly male hops toward a female and offers her a berry. The female accepts the berry and hops away, then stops, and hops back toward the male to offer him the berry in return. • These late nesters can be found throughout Ontario in summer.

Other ID: brown upperparts; yellow wash on belly; grey rump; white undertail coverts.
Size: *L* 18 cm; *W* 30 cm.
Voice: faint, high-pitched, trilled whistle: *tseee-tseee-tseee.*
Status: very common migrant and breeder; uncommon visitor in winter.
Habitat: wooded residential parks and gardens, overgrown fields, forest edges, second-growth, riparian and open woodlands.

Similar Birds

Bohemian Waxwing

Look For

The Bohemian Waxwing (*B. garrulus*) is a cousin of the Cedar Waxwing, but nests in remote northern areas of the province.

cinnamon
head crest

black "mask"

small red "drops"
on wings

yellow terminal
tail band

Nesting: In a coniferous or deciduous tree or shrub; cup nest is made of twigs, moss and lichen; darkly spotted, bluish to greyish eggs are 22 × 16 mm; female incubates 3–5 eggs for 12–16 days.

Did You Know?

The Cedar Waxwing may show signs of tipsiness after eating too many fermented berries, most of which are poisonous to humans. The yellowtail band and "waxy" red wing tips of this bird are a result of pigments in the berries they consume.

Yellow Warbler
Dendroica petechia

The Yellow Warbler is often parasitized by the Brown-headed Cowbird and can recognize cowbird eggs, but rather than tossing them out, will build another nest overtop the old eggs or abandon the nest completely. Occasionally, cowbirds strike repeatedly—a stack of five warbler nests was once found! • The widely distributed Yellow Warbler arrives in May singing its *sweet-sweet* song. These bright yellow birds are often mistakenly called "Wild Canaries." • The Yellow Warbler flits from branch to branch in search of juicy caterpillars, aphids and beetles.

Other ID: yellowish legs; black bill and eyes.
Female: may have faint, red breast streaks.
Size: *L* 13 cm; *W* 20 cm.
Voice: song is a fast, frequently repeated *sweet-sweet-sweet summer sweet.*
Status: common migrant and breeder in spring and summer; may remain into November.
Habitat: moist, open woodlands with dense, low scrub; shrubby meadows, willow tangles, shrubby fencerows and riparian woodlands; usually near water.

Similar Birds

Orange-crowned
Warbler

American
Goldfinch

Common
Yellowthroat (p. 154)

Wilson's
Warbler

bright yellow body

red breast streaks on male

breeding

olive tail and wings with bright yellow barring

Nesting: in a deciduous tree or shrub; female builds a cup nest of grass, weeds and shredded bark; darkly speckled, greyish or greenish white eggs are 17 × 13 mm; female incubates eggs for 11–12 days.

Did You Know?

The Yellow Warbler has an amazing geographical range. It is found throughout North America and on islands in Central and South America.

Look For

In its fall plumage, the male has a flash of yellow on the sides of its tail to distinguish it from other similar-looking warblers.

American Redstart
Setophaga ruticilla

Known as "Butterfly Bird" in some parts of its range, the American Redstart rarely, if ever, sits still. Its Latin American name, *candelita,* meaning "little torch," also describes it perfectly. Not only are the male's bright orange patches the colour of a glowing flame, but the bird never ceases to flicker, even when perched. • In its seemingly nonstop pursuit of prey, the American Redstart flushes insects with a flash of colour from its wings or tail and uses its broad bill and handy, whiskerlike rictal bristles to capture insects like an expert flycatcher.

Other ID: *Male:* white belly and undertail coverts. *Female:* olive brown upperparts; white underparts.
Size: L 13 cm; W 19 cm.
Voice: male's song is a highly variable series of *tseet* or *zee* notes at different pitches; call is a sharp, sweet *chip*.
Status: common migrant and breeder; a few remain into November.
Habitat: shrubby woodland edges, open and semi-open deciduous and mixed forests with a regenerating deciduous understorey of shrubs and saplings; often near water.

Similar Birds

Baltimore Oriole (p. 176)   Orchard Oriole

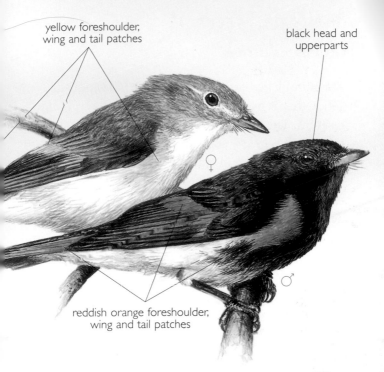

yellow foreshoulder,
wing and tail patches

black head and
upperparts

♀

♂

reddish orange foreshoulder,
wing and tail patches

Nesting: in a shrub or sapling; female builds open cup nest of plant down, bark shreds, grass and rootlets; brown-marked, whitish eggs are 16 x 12 mm; female incubates 4 eggs for 11–12 days.

Did You Know?

Ontario's Point Pelee National Park is an internationally recognized staging site for migrant wood-warblers.

Look For

The colour-splashed tail of the American Redstart sways rhythmically back and forth while it is perched.

Common Yellowthroat

Geothlypis trichas

The bumblebee colours of the male Common Yellowthroat help to identify this skulking wetland resident. The cattail outposts on which he perches to sing his *witchety* song are strategically chosen, and he visits them in rotation, fiercely guarding his territory against the intrusion of other males. • The female wears no "mask" and remains mostly hidden from view in thick vegetation when she tends to the nest.

Other ID: black bill; yellow undertail coverts; orangy legs. *Female:* may show faint, white eye ring.
Size: L 11–14 cm; W 17 cm.
Voice: song is a clear, oscillating *witchety witchety witchety-witch;* call is a sharp *tcheck* or *tchet.*
Status: very common migrant and breeder; a few may remain as late as January.
Habitat: cattail marshes, sedge wetlands, riparian areas, beaver ponds and wet, overgrown meadows; sometimes dry fields.

Similar Birds

Kentucky Warbler

Wilson's Warbler

Nashville Warbler

olive green to olive brown upperparts

♀

dingy white belly

broad, black "mask" with white upper border

yellow throat and breast

♂

Nesting: on or near the ground, in a small shrub or emergent vegetation; female builds an open cup nest of weeds, grass, bark strips and moss; white eggs with dark markings are 17 x 13 mm; female incubates 3–5 eggs for 12 days.

Did You Know?

These birds appear in Ontario from May to September and some-times remain into winter.

Look For

Listen for the call of Common Yellowthroats among those of Marsh Wrens, Red-winged Blackbirds and Pied-billed Grebes.

Scarlet Tanager
Piranga olivacea

The vibrant red of a breeding male Scarlet Tanager may catch your eye in Ontario's wooded ravines and migrant stopover sites. Because this tanager is more likely to reside in forest canopies, birders tend to hear this tanager before they see it. Its song, sort of a slurred version of the American Robin's, is a much-anticipated sound that announces the arrival of this long-distance migrant. • The Scarlet Tanager has the northern-most breeding grounds and longest migration route of all tanager species, and it is the only tanager that routinely nests in Ontario.

Other ID: *Female:* yellow underparts; greyish brown wings; yellow eye ring.
Size: *L* 18 cm; *W* 29 cm.
Voice: song is a series of 4–5 sweet, clear, whistled phrases; call is *chip-burrr* or *chip-churrr.*
Status: uncommon to fairly common migrant; fairly common breeder.
Habitat: fairly mature, upland deciduous and mixed forests.

Similar Birds

Summer Tanager   Northern Cardinal   Baltimore Oriole   Orchard Oriole
               (p. 164)   (p. 176)

olive upperparts

pale bill

♀

♂

pure black wings
and tail

bright red body

breeding

Nesting: high in a deciduous tree; female builds a
flimsy, shallow cup nest of grass, weeds and twigs;
brown-spotted, pale blue green eggs are 23 x 16
mm; female incubates 2–5 eggs for 12–14 days.

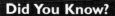

Did You Know?

In Central and South
America, there are over
200 tanager species representing every colour
imaginable.

Look For

Scarlet Tanagers forage in
the forest understorey in
cold, rainy weather, making
them easier to observe.

Chipping Sparrow
Spizella passerina

Though you may spot the relatively tame Chipping Sparrow singing from a high perch, it commonly nests at eye level, so you can easily watch its breeding and nest-building rituals. You can take part in the building of this bird's nest by leaving samples of your pet's hair—or your own—around your backyard. • This bird's song resembles that of the Dark-eyed Junco. Listen for a slightly faster, drier and less musical series of notes to identify the Chipping Sparrow.

Other ID: *Breeding:* mottled brown upperparts; light grey, unstreaked underparts; dark bill. *Nonbreeding:* paler crown with dark streaks; brown "eyebrow" and "cheek"; pale lower mandible.
Size: *L* 13–15 cm; *W* 21 cm.
Voice: song is a rapid, dry trill of *chip* notes; call is a high-pitched *chip*.
Status: uncommon to abundant migrant and breeder; a few overwinter.
Habitat: open conifers or mixed woodland edges; yards and gardens with tree and shrub borders.

Similar Birds

American Tree Sparrow

Swamp Sparrow

Field Sparrow

prominent rufous "cap"

white "eyebrow"

black eye line

white wing bars

breeding

Nesting: usually at midlevel in a coniferous tree; female builds a cup nest of grass and rootlets lined with hair; pale blue, sparsely marked eggs are 18 x 13 mm; female incubates 4 eggs for 11–12 days.

Did You Know?

The Chipping Sparrow is the most common and widely distributed migrating sparrow in North America.

Look For

Chipping Sparrows visit feeders and forage on lawns for the seeds of grass, dandelions and clovers.

Song Sparrow
Melospiza melodia

Although its plumage is unremarkable, the well-named Song Sparrow is among the great songsters of the bird world. By the time a young male Song Sparrow is a few months old, he has created a courtship tune of his own, having learned the basics of melody and rhythm from his father and male rivals. • Mild winters in Ontario usually convince these songsters to stick around. The presence of a well-stocked backyard feeder may be a fair trade for a sweet song in the dead of winter.

Other ID: white jaw line with dark "moustache" stripes; mottled brown upperparts; rounded tail tip.
Size: *L* 14–18 cm; *W* 20 cm.
Voice: song is 1–4 introductory notes, such as *sweet sweet sweet*, followed by buzzy *towee*, then a short, descending trill; call is short *tsip* or *tchep*.
Status: common to abundant migrant and breeder; rare to uncommon winter visitor.
Habitat: willow shrublands, riparian thickets, forest openings and pastures, all often near water.

Similar Birds

Lincoln's Sparrow

Fox Sparrow

Savannah Sparrow

brown line behind eye

dark crown with pale central stripe

greyish face

heavy brown streaks converge at central breast spot

Nesting: usually on the ground or in a low shrub; female builds an open cup nest of grass, weeds and bark strips; brown-blotched, bluish or greenish white eggs are 22 x 17 mm; female incubates 3–5 eggs for 12–14 days.

Did You Know?

Though female songbirds are not usually vocal, the female Song Sparrow will occasionally sing a tune of her own.

Look For

The male Song Sparrow is thought to pump his tail in flight and flutter his wings with his feet dangling for the purpose of attracting a mate.

Dark-eyed Junco
Junco hyemalis

You might feel some sympathy for this sparrow as it picks at scraps under your backyard feeder, but the Dark-eyed Junco prefers to avoid the crowd of noshing chickadees, nuthatches and jays. • The conical shape of the Dark-eyed Junco's bill enables it to use maximum force to crack seeds. • Most juncos migrate south for winter, but even during the coldest years in Ontario, you might find a few lingering "Snow Birds" here.

Other ID: *Female:* grey brown overall.
Size: L 14–17 cm; W 23 cm.
Voice: song is a long, dry trill; call is a smacking *chip* note, often given in series.
Status: common to very common migrant and winter visitor; common breeder.
Habitat: *Breeding:* coniferous and mixed forests; shrubby, regenerating areas. *In migration* and *winter:* shrubby woodland borders, backyard feeders.

Similar Birds

Eastern Towhee

Look For

The Dark-eyed Junco flashes its distinctive white outer tail feathers when it rushes for cover after being flushed.

pale pink bill

dark slate
grey overall

white outer
tail feathers

white belly
and undertail
coverts

♂

"Slate-coloured Junco"

Nesting: on the ground, usually concealed;
female builds a cup nest of twigs, grass, bark
shreds and moss; brown-marked, whitish to bluish
eggs are 19 x 14 mm; female incubates 3–5 eggs
for 12–13 days.

Did You Know?

In 1973, the American Ornithologists' Union grouped five
junco species, all of which interbreed where their ranges
meet, into a single species called the Dark-eyed Junco. The
Ontario subspecies is known as the "Slate-coloured Junco,"

Northern Cardinal
Cardinalis cardinalis

An excited or agitated male Northern Cardinal will display his unforgettable, vibrant red head crest and raise his tail. This colourful year-round resident will vigorously defend his territory, even attacking his own reflection in a window or hubcap! • Cardinals are one of only a few bird species to maintain strong pair bonds. Some couples sing to each other year-round, while others join loose flocks, reestablishing pair bonds in the spring during a "courtship feeding." A male offers a seed to the female, which she then accepts and eats.

Other ID: *Male:* red overall. *Female:* brownish buff overall; fainter "mask"; red crest, wings and tail.
Size: *L* 19–23 cm; *W* 30 cm.
Voice: call is a metallic *chip;* song is series of clear, bubbly whistled notes: *What cheer! What cheer! birdie-birdie-birdie what cheer!*
Status: fairly common to very common year-round resident.
Habitat: brushy thickets and shrubby tangles along forest and woodland edges; backyards and urban and suburban parks.

Similar Birds

Summer Tanager

Scarlet Tanager (p. 156)

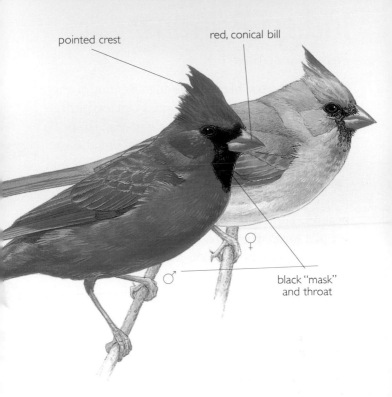

pointed crest

red, conical bill

♀

♂

black "mask" and throat

Nesting: in a dense shrub, vine tangle, or low in a coniferous tree; female builds an open cup nest of twigs, grass and bark shreds; brown-blotched, white to greenish white eggs are 25 x 18 mm; female incubates 3–4 eggs for 12–13 days.

Did You Know?

This bird owes its name to the vivid red plumage of the male, which resembles the robes of Roman Catholic cardinals.

Look For

Northern Cardinals fly with jerky movements and short glides and have a preference for sunflower seeds.

Indigo Bunting
Passerina cyanea

The vivid electric blue male Indigo Bunting is one of the most spectacularly coloured Ontario birds. Indigo Buntings arrive in Ontario in May, choosing raspberry thickets as favoured nesting sites. Dense, thorny stems keep most predators at a distance and the berries are a good food source. • The male is a persistent singer, vocalizing even throughout the heat of a summer day. Young males don't learn their couplet songs from their parents, but from neighbouring males during their first year on their own.

Other ID: beady black eyes; black legs. *Male:* wings and tail may show black or buffy bars; black lores. *Female:* soft brown overall; whitish throat.
Size: *L* 14 cm; *W* 20 cm.
Voice: song consists of paired warbled whistles: *fire-fire, where-where, here-here, see-it see-it;* call is a quick *spit.*
Status: fairly common to common migrant and breeder.
Habitat: deciduous forest and woodland edges, regenerating forest clearings, orchards and shrubby fields.

Similar Birds

Blue Grosbeak

Mountain Bluebird

darker blue head

bright blue overall

grey, conical bill

faint brown streaks on breast

♂

♀

breeding

Nesting: in a small tree, shrub or within a vine tangle; female builds a cup nest of grass, leaves and bark strips; unmarked, white to bluish white eggs are 19 x 14 mm; female incubates 3–4 eggs for 12–13 days.

Did You Know?

The females choose the most melodious males as mates because they are usually the ones that have established territory with the finest habitat.

Look For

The Indigo Bunting lands midway on a stem of grass and shuffles slowly toward the end, bending the stem down to reach the seeds.

Bobolink
Dolichonyx oryzivorus

Originally a prairie species, the Bobolink benefited from the clearing of the eastern deciduous forests and expanded its range eastward to exploit new habitats. • The Bobolink is the most migratory blackbird and the male is coloured like no other bird in Ontario. The female wears more subtle plumage and resembles a sparrow. • A vociferous male Bobolink may defend and mate with several females, but he does not stay for long after the young have hatched.

Other ID: *Breeding male:* white rump and wing patches. *Breeding female:* pale "eyebrow"; dark eye line; whitish throat; streaked back, sides, flank and rump. *Nonbreeding:* similar to female but more yellowish overall.
Size: *L* 15–20 cm; *W* 29 cm.
Voice: song is a series of banjolike twangs: *bobolink bobolink spink spank spink;* call is a musical *pink;* both song and call are given in flight.
Status: common migrant and breeder.
Habitat: tall, grassy meadows and ditches, hayfields and croplands.

Similar Birds

Savannah Sparrow

Grasshopper Sparrow

Vesper Sparrow

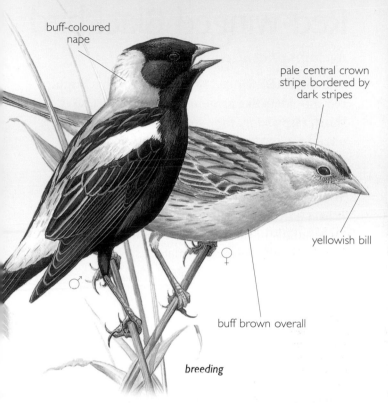

buff-coloured nape

pale central crown stripe bordered by dark stripes

yellowish bill

buff brown overall

♀

♂

breeding

Nesting: well concealed on the ground, usually in a hayfield; female builds a cup nest of grass and weed stems; boldly marked, bluish grey to cinnamon eggs are 22 x 16 mm; female incubates 5–6 eggs for 11–13 days.

Did You Know?

The Bobolink makes a round-trip voyage of up to 20,000 km from its northern breeding grounds to Brazil and Argentina and back again.

Look For

The Bobolink arrives in Ontario in late April and stays until September.

Red-winged Blackbird

Agelaius phoeniceus

The male Red-winged Blackbird wears his bright red shoulders like armour—together with his short, raspy song, they are key to defending his territory from rivals. In field experiments, males whose red shoulders were painted black soon lost their territories. • These birds are early spring arrivals, often returning to Ontario in mid-March. It isn't hard to spot the polygynous males perched atop cattails in roadside ditches and wetlands, but the cryptically coloured females usually remain inconspicuous on their nests.

Other ID: *Male:* black overall. *Female:* mottled brown upperparts; pale "eyebrow."
Size: *L* 18–24 cm; *W* 33 cm.
Voice: song is a loud, raspy *konk-a-ree* or *ogle-reeeee;* calls include a harsh *check* and high *tseert;* female gives a loud *che-che-che chee chee chee.*
Status: abundant migrant and breeder; rare to fairly common, local winter visitor.
Habitat: cattail marshes, wet meadows and ditches, croplands and shoreline shrubs.

Similar Birds

Rusty Blackbird

Brown-headed Cowbird (p. 174)

Brewer's Blackbird

faint, red
shoulder patch

red shoulder
patch edged
in yellow

♂

♀

heavily streaked
underparts

Nesting: colonial; in cattails or shoreline bushes; female builds an open cup nest of dried cattail leaves lined with fine grass; darkly marked, pale blue green to grey eggs are 25 x 18 mm; female incubates 3–4 eggs for 10–12 days.

Did You Know?

Some scientists believe that the Red-winged Blackbird is the most abundant bird of any species in North America.

Look For

Red-winged Blackbirds gather in immense flocks in agricultural areas and open fields in winter.

Eastern Meadowlark
Sturnella magna

The drab dress of most female songbirds lends them and their nestlings protection during the breeding season, but the female Eastern Meadowlark uses a different strategy. She shares the V-shaped necklace and bright yellow throat and belly of her male counterpart, but for a slightly different purpose—an incubating female will burst from the grass, creating a colourful distraction to lead predators away from the nest. • Listen for this bird's proud song whistled from the fence posts and powerlines of rural Ontario.

Other ID: yellow lores; dark crown stripes and eye line; pale "eyebrow"; dark streaking on white sides and flanks.
Size: L 23–24 cm; W 35 cm.
Voice: song is a rich series of 2–8 melodic, slurred whistles: *see-you at school-today* or *this is the year;* gives a rattling flight call and a high, buzzy *dzeart.*
Status: uncommon to common migrant and breeder; rare visitor in winter.
Habitat: grassy meadows and pastures, croplands, weedy fields, grassy roadsides and old orchards.

Similar Birds

Western Meadowlark

Dickcissel

mottled brown
upperparts

long, sharp bill

short, wide tail
with white outer
tail feathers

broad, black
breast band

yellow
underparts

long,
pinkish legs

breeding

Nesting: in a concealed depression on the ground; female builds a domed grass nest, woven into surrounding vegetation; heavily spotted, white eggs are 28 x 20 mm; female incubates 3–7 eggs for 13–15 days.

Did You Know?

Though its name suggests that this bird is a lark, it is actually a member of the blackbird family. Its silhouette reveals its blackbird features.

Look For

The Eastern Meadowlark is easily confused with the very similar-looking, but rare Western Meadowlark. Listen for their different songs to distinguish them.

Brown-headed Cowbird
Molothrus ater

Brown-headed Cowbirds are best described as pests. These nomads historically followed bison herds across the prairies and they do not build their own nests. Instead, they lay their eggs in other birds' nests to be incubated and their aggressive young to be fed by other unsuspecting mothers. Orioles, warblers, vireos and tanagers are among the most affected. Increased livestock farming and fragmentation of forests has encouraged the expansion of the cowbird's range and it now parasitizes more than 140 bird species.

Other ID: thick, conical bill; short, squared tail.
Size: *L* 15–20 cm; *W* 30 cm.
Voice: song is a high, liquidy gurgle: *glug-ahl-whee* or *bubbloozeee;* call is a squeaky, high-pitched *seep, psee* or *wee-tse-tse* or fast, chipping *ch-ch-ch-ch-ch-ch.*
Status: very common migrant and breeder; rare to locally common winter visitor.
Habitat: agricultural fields, woodland edges, utility cutlines, roadsides, fencelines, landfills, campgrounds and areas near cattle.

Similar Birds

Brewer's Blackbird

Rusty Blackbird

Common Grackle

dark eyes

pale throat

dark brown head

light brown underparts
with faint streaking

♀

♂

iridescent, green blue body
plumage looks glossy black

Nesting: does not build a nest; female lays up to 40 eggs a year in the nests of other birds, usually 1 egg per nest; brown-speckled, whitish eggs are 21 x 16 mm; eggs hatch after 10–13 days.

Did You Know?

These birds do not form pair bonds, but the male does fan his tail and wings in a form of courtship display.

Look For

When cowbirds feed in flocks, they hold their back ends up high, with their tails sticking straight up in the air.

Baltimore Oriole
Icterus galbula

With a robinlike song and a preference for the canopies of your neighbourhood trees, the Baltimore Oriole is difficult to spot, and a hanging pouch nest dangling in a bare tree in fall is sometimes the only evidence the bird was there at all. Orioles spend more than half of each year in the tropics of Central and South America, but breed in Ontario. Very few of these birds stay for winter, but you might spot one in its Hallowe'en colours lingering at a feeder, especially one that offers orange halves.

Other ID: *Male:* black upperparts. *Female:* olive brown upperparts (darkest on head). *In flight:* male's orange tail has black base and central stripe.
Size: *L* 18–20 cm; *W* 29 cm.
Voice: song consists of slow, clear whistles: *peter peter peter here peter;* calls include a 2-note *tea-too* and a rapid chatter: *ch-ch-ch-ch-ch.*
Status: uncommon to common migrant and breeder; a few remain in winter.
Habitat: deciduous and mixed forests, particularly riparian woodlands, natural openings, shorelines, roadsides, orchards, gardens and parklands.

Similar Birds

Orchard Oriole

Summer Tanager

Scarlet Tanager (p. 156)

2 white
wing bands

white wing band
and feather edgings

dull yellow
orange under-
parts and rump

bright orange
underparts

Nesting: high in a deciduous tree; female builds a hanging pouch nest of grass, bark shreds and grapevines, occasionally adding string; darkly marked, pale grey to bluish white eggs are 23 x 15 mm; female incubates 4–5 eggs for 12–14 days.

Did You Know?

The male Baltimore Oriole's breeding colours mirror the coat of arms of George Calvert, the Irishman who established the first colony in Maryland.

Look For

The Baltimore Oriole inhabits Ontario from May to early October.

Purple Finch

Carpodacus purpureus

Despite its name, the Purple Finch's stunning plumage is more raspberry red rather than purple. Its musical *pik* call is given frequently and is a good way to know if this finch is nearby. A flat, raised, table-style feeding station and nearby tree cover are sure to attract Purple Finches, and a feeder may keep a small flock in your area over winter. • In breeding season, the male dances around the female, beating his wings rapidly until he gracefully lifts into the air.

Other ID: notched tail. *Male:* reddish brown "cheek"; brown streaking on back and flanks; red rump. *Female:* dark brown "cheek" and "jawline"; grey brown upperparts with whitish streaks.
Size: L 13–15 cm; W 25 cm.
Voice: song is a bubbly, continuous warble; call is a single metallic *pik*.
Status: fairly common migrant and breeder; rare to locally uncommon visitor in winter.
Habitat: *Breeding:* coniferous and mixed forests. *In migration* and *winter:* coniferous, mixed and deciduous forests, shrubby open areas and feeders.

Similar Birds

House Finch

Red Crossbill

white "eyebrow" and lower "cheek" stripe

raspberry red wash over most of body

heavily streaked underparts

♀

pale, conical bill

pale, unstreaked underparts

♂

Nesting: on a conifer branch, far from the trunk; female builds a cup nest of twigs, grass and rootlets; darkly marked, pale greenish blue eggs are 20 x 15 mm; female incubates 4–5 eggs for 13 days.

Did You Know?

Purple Finches are especially fond of red maple, apple and elm flowers in spring.

Look For

The male often delivers his song from an exposed perch at the top of a live tree.

Common Redpoll
Carduelis flammea

These tiny snowplows sometimes make a modest appearance, showing up in winter in Ontario in small groups of a dozen or less. Other winters, they flock in the hundreds, gleaning waste grain from bare fields or stocking up at winter feeders. • A large surface area relative to their small internal volume puts Common Redpolls at risk of freezing in cold temperatures, but an insulating layer of warm air created by their fluffed feathers and their high intake of food keep these songbirds from dying of hypothermia.

Other ID: yellowish bill; streaked upperparts; notched tail.
Size: *L* 13 cm; W 22 cm.
Voice: song is a twittering series of trills; calls are a soft *chit-chit-chit-chit* and a faint *swe-eet*.
Status: fairly common year-round resident and breeder; uncommon to locally abundant, irruptive winter visitor.
Habitat: open fields and meadows; along roadsides, utility power lines, railways, forest edges; backyards with feeders.

Similar Birds

Hoary Redpoll

Pine Siskin

red forecrown

black "chin"

lightly
streaked sides

pinkish red
breast on male

flanks and
undertail coverts

♀

♂

nonbreeding

Nesting: low in a shrub or dwarf spruce; occasionally in a grass clump; open cup nest is made of fine twigs, grass and moss; darkly speckled, pale blue eggs are 17 x 13 mm; female incubates 4–5 eggs for 12 days.

Did You Know?

Common Redpolls can endure colder temperatures than any other songbird.

Look For

Common Redpolls spend a lot of time at feeders in the winter and prefer birch and alder seeds because of their high calorie content.

House Sparrow
Passer domesticus

A black "mask" and "bib" adorn the male of this adaptive, aggressive species. The House Sparrow's tendency to usurp territory has led to a decline in native bird populations. This sparrow will even help itself to the convenience of another bird's home, such as a bluebird's nest or a Purple Martin house. • Male House Sparrows with larger "bibs" are thought to attract a mate more easily. When a pair bond is established it is maintained throughout the breeding season.

Other ID: *Breeding male:* black lores and "bib"; grey crown; black bill; dark, mottled upperparts; white wing bar. *Female:* indistinct facial patterns; plain grey brown overall; streaked upperparts.
Size: *L* 14–17 cm; *W* 24 cm.
Voice: song is a plain, familiar *cheep-cheep-cheep-cheep;* call is a short *chill-up.*
Status: abundant year-round resident.
Habitat: townsites, urban and suburban areas, farmyards and agricultural areas, railway yards and other developed areas.

Similar Birds

Harris's Sparrow

Look For

In spring, House Sparrows feast on the buds of fruit trees. In winter, these birds flock together in barns in rural areas and at garbage dumps in cities.

buffy "eyebrow"

greyish, unstreaked underparts

chestnut nape

light grey "cheek"

♀

grey underparts

♂

breeding

Nesting: often communal; in a human-made structure, ornamental shrub or natural cavity; pair builds a large dome nest of grass, twigs and plant fibres; variably marked white to greenish eggs are 23 x 16 mm; pair incubates 4–6 eggs for 10–13 days.

Did You Know?

House Sparrows are not closely related to the other North American sparrows, but belong to the family of Old World sparrows or "Weaver Finches." They were introduced to North America in the 1850s as part of a plan to control the insects that were damaging grain and cereal crops. As it turns out, these birds are largely vegetarian!

Glossary

accipiter: a forest hawk (genus *Accipiter*), characterized by a long tail and short, rounded wings; feeds mostly on birds.

brood: *n.* a family of young from one hatching; *v.* to incubate the eggs.

brood parasite: a bird that lays its eggs in other birds' nests.

buteo: a high-soaring hawk (genus *Buteo*), characterized by broad wings and a short, wide tail; feeds mostly on small mammals and other land animals.

cere: on birds of prey, a fleshy area at the base of the bill that contains the nostrils.

clutch: the number of eggs laid by the female at one time.

dabbling: a foraging technique used by some ducks, in which the head and neck are submerged but the body and tail remain on the water's surface; dabbling ducks can usually walk easily on land, can take off without running and have brightly coloured speculums.

"eclipse" plumage: a cryptic plumage, similar to that of females, worn by some male ducks in autumn when they moult their flight feathers and consequently are unable to fly.

flushing: when frightened birds explode into flight in response to a disturbance.

flycatching: a feeding behaviour in which the bird leaves a perch, snatches an insect in mid-air and returns to the same perch; also known as "hawking" or "sallying."

pelagic: refers to birds that inhabit the ocean very far from land.

precocial: a bird that is relatively well developed at hatching; precocial birds usually have open eyes, extensive down and are fairly mobile.

riparian: refers to habitat along riverbanks.

sexual dimorphism: a difference in plumage, size, or other characteristics between males and females of the same species.

speculum: a brightly coloured patch on the wings of many dabbling ducks.

stage: to gather in one place during migration, usually when birds are flightless or partly flightless during moulting.

stoop: a steep dive through the air, usually performed by birds of prey while foraging or during courtship displays.

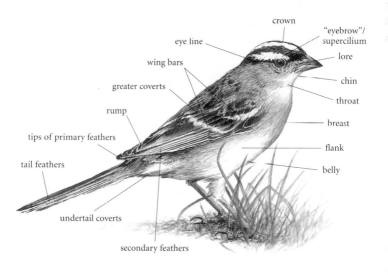

Checklist

The following checklist contains 319 species of birds that are regularly seen in Ontario. Species are grouped by family and listed in taxonomic order in accordance with the A.O.U. *Check-list of North American Birds* (7th ed.) and its supplements. In addition, the following COSEWIC (Committee on the Status of Endangered Wildlife in Canada) risk categories are also noted: endangered (en), threatened (th) and special concern (sc).

Waterfowl
❑ Greater White-fronted Goose
❑ Snow Goose
❑ Ross's Goose
❑ Cackling Goose
❑ Canada Goose
❑ Brant
❑ Mute Swan
❑ Trumpeter Swan
❑ Tundra Swan
❑ Wood Duck
❑ Gadwall
❑ Eurasian Wigeon
❑ American Wigeon
❑ American Black Duck
❑ Mallard
❑ Blue-winged Teal
❑ Northern Shoveler
❑ Northern Pintail
❑ Green-winged Teal
❑ Canvasback
❑ Redhead
❑ Ring-necked Duck
❑ Greater Scaup
❑ Lesser Scaup
❑ King Eider
❑ Common Eider
❑ Harlequin Duck
❑ Surf Scoter
❑ White-winged Scoter
❑ Black Scoter
❑ Long-tailed Duck
❑ Bufflehead
❑ Common Goldeneye
❑ Barrow's Goldeneye
❑ Hooded Merganser
❑ Common Merganser
❑ Red-breasted Merganser
❑ Ruddy Duck

Grouse & Allies
❑ Gray Partridge
❑ Ring-necked Pheasant
❑ Ruffed Grouse
❑ Spruce Grouse
❑ Willow Ptarmigan
❑ Sharp-tailed Grouse
❑ Wild Turkey

New World Quail
❑ Northern Bobwhite (en)

Loons
❑ Red-throated Loon
❑ Pacific Loon
❑ Common Loon

Grebes
❑ Pied-billed Grebe
❑ Horned Grebe
❑ Red-necked Grebe
❑ Eared Grebe

Pelicans
❑ American White Pelican

Cormorants
❑ Double-crested Cormorant

Herons
- ❑ American Bittern
- ❑ Least Bittern (th)
- ❑ Great Blue Heron
- ❑ Great Egret
- ❑ Snowy Egret
- ❑ Cattle Egret
- ❑ Green Heron
- ❑ Black-crowned
  Night-Heron

Vultures
- ❑ Turkey Vulture

Kites, Hawks & Eagles
- ❑ Osprey
- ❑ Bald Eagle
- ❑ Northern Harrier
- ❑ Sharp-shinned Hawk
- ❑ Cooper's Hawk
- ❑ Northern Goshawk
- ❑ Red-shouldered Hawk (sc)
- ❑ Broad-winged Hawk
- ❑ Red-tailed Hawk
- ❑ Rough-legged Hawk
- ❑ Golden Eagle

Falcons
- ❑ American Kestrel
- ❑ Merlin
- ❑ Gyrfalcon
- ❑ Peregrine Falcon (th)

Rails & Coots
- ❑ Yellow Rail (sc)
- ❑ King Rail (en)
- ❑ Virginia Rail
- ❑ Sora
- ❑ Common Moorhen
- ❑ American Coot

Cranes
- ❑ Sandhill Crane

Plovers
- ❑ Black-bellied Plover
- ❑ American Golden-Plover
- ❑ Semipalmated Plover
- ❑ Piping Plover (en)
- ❑ Killdeer

Sandpipers & Allies
- ❑ Greater Yellowlegs
- ❑ Lesser Yellowlegs
- ❑ Solitary Sandpiper
- ❑ Willet
- ❑ Spotted Sandpiper
- ❑ Upland Sandpiper
- ❑ Whimbrel
- ❑ Hudsonian Godwit
- ❑ Marbled Godwit
- ❑ Ruddy Turnstone
- ❑ Red Knot
- ❑ Sanderling
- ❑ Semipalmated Sandpiper
- ❑ Western Sandpiper
- ❑ Least Sandpiper
- ❑ White-rumped Sandpiper
- ❑ Baird's Sandpiper
- ❑ Pectoral Sandpiper
- ❑ Purple Sandpiper
- ❑ Dunlin
- ❑ Stilt Sandpiper
- ❑ Buff-breasted Sandpiper
- ❑ Ruff
- ❑ Short-billed Dowitcher
- ❑ Long-billed Dowitcher
- ❑ Wilson's Snipe
- ❑ American Woodcock
- ❑ Wilson's Phalarope
- ❑ Red-necked Phalarope
- ❑ Red Phalarope

Gulls & Allies
- ❑ Pomarine Jaeger
- ❑ Parasitic Jaeger
- ❑ Long-tailed Jaeger
- ❑ Laughing Gull
- ❑ Franklin's Gull
- ❑ Little Gull
- ❑ Black-headed Gull
- ❑ Bonaparte's Gull
- ❑ Ring-billed Gull
- ❑ Herring Gull
- ❑ Thayer's Gull
- ❑ Iceland Gull
- ❑ Lesser Black-backed Gull
- ❑ Glaucous Gull
- ❑ Great Black-backed Gull

❏ Sabine's Gull
❏ Black-legged Kittiwake
❏ Caspian Tern
❏ Common Tern
❏ Arctic Tern
❏ Forster's Tern
❏ Black Tern

Pigeons & Doves
❏ Rock Pigeon
❏ Mourning Dove

Cuckoos
❏ Black-billed Cuckoo
❏ Yellow-billed Cuckoo

Owls
❏ Eastern Screech-Owl
❏ Great Horned Owl
❏ Snowy Owl
❏ Northern Hawk Owl
❏ Barred Owl
❏ Great Gray Owl
❏ Long-eared Owl
❏ Short-eared Owl (sc)
❏ Boreal Owl
❏ Northern Saw-Whet Owl

Nightjars
❏ Common Nighthawk
❏ Chuck-will's-widow
❏ Whip-poor-will

Swifts
❏ Chimney Swift

Hummingbirds
❏ Ruby-throated
  Hummingbird

Kingfishers
❏ Belted Kingfisher

Woodpeckers
❏ Red-headed Woodpecker (sc)
❏ Red-bellied Woodpecker
❏ Yellow-bellied Sapsucker
❏ Downy Woodpecker
❏ Hairy Woodpecker
❏ American Three-toed
  Woodpecker
❏ Black-backed Woodpeker

❏ Northern Flicker
❏ Pileated Woodpecker

Flycatchers
❏ Olive-sided Flycatcher
❏ Eastern Wood-Pewee
❏ Yellow-bellied Flycatcher
❏ Acadian Flycatcher (en)
❏ Alder Flycatcher
❏ Willow Flycatcher
❏ Least Flycatcher
❏ Eastern Phoebe
❏ Great Crested Flycatcher
❏ Western Kingbird
❏ Eastern Kingbird

Shrikes
❏ Loggerhead Shrike (en)
❏ Northern Shrike

Vireos
❏ White-eyed Vireo
❏ Yellow-throated Vireo
❏ Blue-headed Vireo
❏ Warbling Vireo
❏ Philadelphia Vireo
❏ Red-eyed Vireo

Jays & Crows
❏ Gray Jay
❏ Blue Jay
❏ Black-billed Magpie
❏ American Crow
❏ Common Raven

Larks
❏ Horned Lark

Swallows
❏ Purple Martin
❏ Tree Swallow
❏ Northern Rough-winged
  Swallow
❏ Bank Swallow
❏ Cliff Swallow
❏ Barn Swallow

Chickadees & Titmice
❏ Black-capped Chickadee
❏ Boreal Chickadee
❏ Tufted Titmouse

Nuthatches
❑ Red-breasted Nuthatch
❑ White-breasted Nuthatch

Creepers
❑ Brown Creeper

Wrens
❑ Carolina Wren
❑ House Wren
❑ Winter Wren
❑ Sedge Wren
❑ Marsh Wren

Kinglets
❑ Golden-crowned Kinglet
❑ Ruby-crowned Kinglet

Gnatcatchers
❑ Blue-gray Gnatcatcher

Thrushes
❑ Eastern Bluebird
❑ Veery
❑ Gray-cheeked Thrush
❑ Swainson's Thrush
❑ Hermit Thrush
❑ Wood Thrush
❑ American Robin
❑ Varied Thrush

Mimics & Thrashers
❑ Gray Catbird
❑ Northern Mockingbird
❑ Brown Thrasher

Starlings
❑ European Starling

Pipits
❑ American Pipit

Waxwings
❑ Bohemian Waxwing
❑ Cedar Waxwing

Wood-Warblers
❑ Blue-winged Warbler
❑ Golden-winged Warbler
❑ Tennessee Warbler
❑ Orange-crowned Warbler
❑ Nashville Warbler
❑ Northern Parula

❑ Yellow Warbler
❑ Chestnut-sided Warbler
❑ Magnolia Warbler
❑ Cape May Warbler
❑ Black-throated Blue Warbler
❑ Yellow-rumped Warbler
❑ Black-throated Green Warbler
❑ Blackburnian Warbler
❑ Yellow-throated Warbler
❑ Pine Warbler
❑ Prairie Warbler
❑ Palm Warbler
❑ Bay-breasted Warbler
❑ Blackpoll Warbler
❑ Cerulean Warbler (sc)
❑ Black-and-white Warbler
❑ American Redstart
❑ Prothonotary Warbler (en)
❑ Worm-eating Warbler
❑ Ovenbird
❑ Northern Waterthrush
❑ Louisiana Waterthrush (sc)
❑ Kentucky Warbler
❑ Connecticut Warbler
❑ Mourning Warbler
❑ Common Yellowthroat
❑ Hooded Warbler (th)
❑ Wilson's Warbler
❑ Canada Warbler
❑ Yellow-breasted Chat (sc)

Tanagers
❑ Summer Tanager
❑ Scarlet Tanager

Sparrows & Allies
❑ Eastern Towhee
❑ American Tree Sparrow
❑ Chipping Sparrow
❑ Clay-colored Sparrow
❑ Field Sparrow
❑ Vesper Sparrow
❑ Savannah Sparrow
❑ Grasshopper Sparrow
❑ Henslow's Sparrow (en)
❑ Le Conte's Sparrow
❑ Nelson's Sharp-tailed Sparrow
❑ Fox Sparrow

- ❏ Song Sparrow
- ❏ Lincoln's Sparrow
- ❏ Swamp Sparrow
- ❏ White-throated Sparrow
- ❏ Harris's Sparrow
- ❏ White-crowned Sparrow
- ❏ Dark-eyed Junco
- ❏ Lapland Longspur
- ❏ Smith's Longspur
- ❏ Snow Bunting

Grosbeaks & Buntings
- ❏ Northern Cardinal
- ❏ Rose-breasted Grosbeak
- ❏ Blue Grosbeak
- ❏ Indigo Bunting
- ❏ Dickcissel

Blackbirds & Allies
- ❏ Bobolink
- ❏ Red-winged Blackbird
- ❏ Eastern Meadowlark
- ❏ Western Meadowlark

- ❏ Yellow-headed Blackbird
- ❏ Rusty Blackbird
- ❏ Brewer's Blackbird
- ❏ Common Grackle
- ❏ Brown-headed Cowbird
- ❏ Orchard Oriole
- ❏ Baltimore Oriole

Finches
- ❏ Pine Grosbeak
- ❏ Purple Finch
- ❏ House Finch
- ❏ Red Crossbill
- ❏ White-winged Crossbill
- ❏ Common Redpoll
- ❏ Hoary Redpoll
- ❏ Pine Siskin
- ❏ American Goldfinch
- ❏ Evening Grosbeak

Old World Sparrows
- ❏ House Sparrow

Select References

American Ornithologists' Union. 1998. *Check-list of North American Birds.* 7th ed. (and its supplements). American Ornithologists' Union, Washington, D.C.

Butler, Elaine. 1991. *Attracting Birds.* Lone Pine Publishing, Edmonton, Alberta.

Elphick, C., J. B. Dunning, Jr., and D.A. Sibley, eds. 2001. *National Audubon Society The Sibley Guide to Bird Life & Behavior.* Alfred A. Knopf, New York.

Roth, Sally. 1998. *Attracting Birds to Your Backyard 536 Ways to Turn Your Yard and Garden into a Haven for Your Favorite Birds.* Rodale Press, Inc. Emmaus, Pennsylvania.

Sibley, D. A. 2000. *National Audubon Society: The Sibley Guide to Birds.* Alfred A. Knopf, New York.

Index